Poetry Ireland Review 75

Eagarthóir / Editor **Michael Smith**

Poetry Ireland Ltd./Éigse Éireann Teo. gratefully acknowledges the assistance of The Arts Council/An Chomhairle Ealaíon, the Arts Council of Northern Ireland, and FÁS.

Patrons of Poetry Ireland/Éigse Éireann

Grogan's Castle Lounge	Desmond Windle
Dr. G. Rosenstock	Joan & Joe McBreen
Eastern Washington University	Dillon Murphy & Co.
Fearon, O'Neill, Rooney	Office Of Public Works
Daig Quinn	Richard Murphy
Twomey Steo Ltd.	Occidental Tourist Ltd.
Kevin Connolly	Winding Stair Bookshop
Neville Keery	Doirín Meagher
The Irish-American Poetry Society	Swan Training Institute

Poetry Ireland invites individuals, cultural groups and commercial organisations to become Patrons. Patrons are entitled to reclaim tax at their highest rate for all donations of between €128.00 and €12,700. For more details please contact the Director, at Bermingham Tower, Dublin Castle, Dublin 2, Ireland or phone 01 6714632 or e-mail: **management@poetryireland.ie**

ISSN: 0332-2998
ISBN: 1-902121-13-9

Assistant Editor: Paul Lenehan
Cover Template: Colm Ó Cannain
Typography: Barry Hannigan
Cover Photo: 'Curlew Skull' by Hugh McElveen (see **Notes on Contributors**).

Printed in Ireland by **ColourBooks Ltd.**, Baldoyle Industrial Estate, Dublin13.

Contents

Poetry Ireland Review 75

	3	Editorial
Paul Muldoon	5	The Treaty
Eoghan Ó Tuairisc		Three sections from 'Aifreann na Marbh'
	6	1. Introit
	7	2. Kyrie
	10	3. Gradual
Rita Ann Higgins	11	They Had No Song
Mary O'Donnell	12	Turn, season
Jan Conn	13	Near the Solimões River, 1880
	13	Bowl and Spear
Arturo Carrera	14	Frogs
Hugh O'Donnell	16	Soap Opera
David Butler	17	Millennium
Augustus Young	18	Brine Breath
PJ McNally	19	Beg-Meil
Paul Murray	20	The Seagulls in the City

Feature on Palestinian Poetry

Mahoud Darwish	23	*from* A State of Siege
Fadwa Tuqan	26	To Christ the Lord on His Birthday
Mourid Barghouti	28	Snow Poem
Sharif S Elmusa	30	Homeward Bound
Jabra Ibrahim Jabra	32	Love's Kingdom
Zakaria Mohammed	35	Sun Stroke
	37	A House
	38	The Reapers
Ghassan Zaqtan	39	The Road in Darkness
	40	Four Sisters from Zakariya
	41	Beirut, August 1982

Winners / Runners-Up in the *SeaCat National Poetry Competition 2002* in association with *Poetry Ireland*

Marianne Hennessy	42	Airport After Hours
Manus Joseph McManus	44	Snow
Michael Clement	45	My Father Loved Pigeons
Celia de Fréine	46	Grace
Michael Coady	48	Thirteen Souls with Bread and Wine
John O'Donnell	50	The Majestic

Mary O'Donnell   51   Poetry in Crisis?

Maurice Harmon   57   The Era of Disappointment

James J McAuley   66   Five Firsts

Michael S Begnal   73   Gràdh, Grá, Grá

David Butler   78   Four Debuts and a Reappearance

Brian Coffey   82   Of Denis Devlin: Vestiges,
                             Sentences, Presages

Dennis O'Driscoll   101   Pickings & Choosings

Michael Smith   108   Interview with Thomas Kinsella

                 120   Notes on Contributors

                 123   Books Received

Editorial/Eagarfhocal

This is the third and final issue of *PIR* under my editorship. Like all editorial work, I suppose it bears the impression of my own preferences; but having said that, I would also like to believe that I have tried to maintain standards of excellence as well as generating interest in the world of poetry beyond this island. Indeed, my main intention as editor has been to stimulate interest in the nature of poetry, in its relationship with society both here and abroad and to broaden the minds of readers here in their notions about Irish poetry, so that Irish poets who have been engaged in the development of the possibilities in poetry are not marginalised and treated as freakish and of no consequence. I have never considered that the choice facing an Irish poet was simply between 'the mainstream' and 'the experimental': it has been my view that poetic discourse holds many possibilities, and views that inhibit the exploration of these possibilities are regressive and downright bad for the health of poetry. That, at any rate, is my view of the matter.

The Palestinian poetry included in this issue was not chosen for any political reason. It is not the business of the Editor of *Poetry Ireland Review* to push for any political programme, whatever his or her own political convictions may be. But of course the lives of poets, like those of everyone else, are inevitably affected by the political situations in which their societies find themselves, and for that reason political concerns may find their way into what they write. There is, for example, explicitly propagandist poetry by which the poet deliberately sets out to effect political change through the instrument of poetry. Whether that is justifiable or not is a whole debate in itself, but it is not a debate which I have attempted to provoke in these pages. This does not mean that I hold the view that politics has no place in poetry. There is politics in Shakespeare as there is in Brecht or Pasternak or Seamus Heaney. What matters is that the poetics should not be subservient to the politics, and that the poetics are broad enough in their scope and deep enough in their penetration of the human condition to engage readers as human beings for whom poetry is an importantly and uniquely human discourse.

Erratum: In *Poetry Ireland Review* 74, the date given on Paul Durcan's 'Letter from one Young Poet to Another' was Friday, April 26, 1967. This is incorrect; the date should have read Friday, April 26, 1963, four years earlier.

Michael Smith, Editor

Paul Muldoon

The Treaty

My grandfather, Frank Regan, cross-shanked, his shoulders in a moult,
steadies the buff
of his underparts against the ledge of the chimney-bluff
of the mud-walled house in Cullenramer

in which, earlier, he had broken open a bolt
of the sky-stuff
and held it to the failing light, having himself failed to balance
                              Gormley's cuffs.
"This Collins," Gormley had wagged, "is a right flimflammer."

Cross-shanked against the chimney-bluff, he's sizing up what follows
from our being on the verge
of nation-

hood when another broad-lapelled, swallow-tailed swallow
comes at a clip through the dusk-blue serge
to make some last minute alterations.

Eoghan Ó Tuairisc

Three sections from 'Aifreann na Marbh' (*Lux Aeterna*, 1964)

1. Introit

The morning arouses our unceasing unease.
From behind a pane of glass I look out
At the bell towers of the Adam-clan:
Our slates, our creed, our lawcourts
Floating in the freshness.
Out of the haze
The virginal bright city
Unveils herself for me,
Offering resurrection.
The morning arouses our unceasing unease.

The lonely-sweet pang in my heart
Stirs at the sight of her beauty,
Stretching her limbs, her bright streets,
Beside the river. And the woods
And the line of the trickling hill-peaks
Establish her in her hundred guises,
My girl-city stark naked
Sleeping by the wattle-ford.
The morning arouses our unceasing unease.

The dream-vision out of the east, planet-proud,
Comes and scatters roseate-silver light
Among the grime of her harbour;
Comes as sparkling day, blinding,
And violates her virginity
Till each chimney, each beam
And ship's mast
Is reduced to black bone,
To photographic negative,
Bringing out the meaning of my verse:
The morning arouses our unceasing unease.

– translated by Aidan Hayes with Anna Ní Dhomhnaill

2. Kyrie

Siú Íosasú, amhaireimí tama-i!*

Have mercy on us who are without mercy,
Have pity on our lust for science.
Through the grime of the era
That we ourselves created
Show the new sun.
We split the apple
And left the old sun ash-coated. *Siú Íosasú.*

Amhaireimí, mercy on us who step out briskly
On the streets on a Monday morning,
Blind to the company of our bright shadows
Who peer at us from window-glass:
A second crowd of walkers
Quietly walking in step with our step,
Pale. Dead. Tamed. *Siú Íosasú.*

Siú. I walk. Through the accident of languages
I move on, reflecting on our triumph –
The knowledge of good and evil
Under the control of the uncontrolled one
Like a little god in its progress.
Amhaireimí. Amhaireimí. Siú Íosasú.

In through a university archway,
Breasting the stream of bright young faces,
Bags on shoulders, pushing toward the light,
Discussing space, the latest theorem –
The blonde heads and the red –
Their contribution under mathematics' yoke. *Siú.*

**Lord Jesus, have mercy on us!* (This prayer was heard on the streets of Hiroshima on the morning of the tragedy).

Their freshness stays in the draught their passing makes:
Pausing a moment in the narrow passageway,
The shine and young laughter of the ages
That was stored in fragile sweet speech.
The nymphs stole away from us,
But the honey of their begetting stays
Under this arch of ours. *Siú.*

Through contemporary eyes I look again
At the stubborn stone, the monastic square,
The quiet of the cloister, the circle of its dream-vision
That will not be aroused by the bell,
Nor the mute pain-filled howl of history
That's deep in the heart of the rose that hangs by the wall. *Siú.*

Dates are cited, the names of architects,
The confident discourse of mild-mannered gelded academics.
Not conveyed in passionate words,
The name of the architect of the original arch.
The fatal Monday goes unmentioned
Till the bawdy gravel's voice is heard under our heels. *Siú.*

A piercing roar comes from the playing-field,
Deepening the quiet and bringing home
The sterility of the desert where we are,
Behind our childish masks, hoping
The heavy consequences don't fall on us
Even though the roses are screaming from their fragrant core. *Siú.*

In the solitude of the library I seek answers –
The noble lettering and the otter
Seizing the fish in the codex of Kells.
Between the conception and its crucifixion,
The two secrets binding the conclusion of the work,
The emaciated name of the one I killed. *Siú Íosasú.*

Siú. Walk. I am walking. We are walking
Through conjugations of verbs, the fatal whine,
Onward from Monday to Monday inventing emblems
In the granite blocks of this purposeless city:
The girl-woman stands against it.
Siú Íosasú, amhaireimí tama-i.

                    – translated by Aidan Hayes with Anna Ní Dhomhnaill

3. Gradual

Don't hold it against me O Christ,
That I stole
The form of your bright passion
To fashion my dream-vision.

My soul's anguish,
Standing head uncovered
On the steps of the crucified city,
Is the reason for my thieving.

We are the dead who died
In Dublin and out of season,
On blasphemy's sunny day
We blew away Hiroshima.

We are no longer Gaels from the line of Ir and Éibhir,
The slaughter done in pursuit of Deirdre is no news to us.
Now, by the ship-crowded Liffey in the time of my decline
I see our beginning clear, our ending – we, children of Eve.

– translated by Aidan Hayes with Anna Ní Dhomhnaill

Rita Ann Higgins

They Had No Song

It had all the hallmarks
of something passionate.
It looked real, it sounded real
but in the end as in the beginning
it was nothing more than the dream team
play-acting the big roll, skirting on the outside of devotion
on the rim of lit cities, periphery smiffphery
outside Christmases, inside themselves
making things bigger multiplying when adding would do.

Phones didn't help, too many pauses
one didn't know whether the other was cooing or coming
e-mails were worse more periphery smiffphery
all cryptic and vague nothing ventured nothing stained
no stain no gain, no Sunday afternoons to fuck in
no long weekends made longer by lingus kissus
no bulgaricus on each other's bad habits
no data on his n' her Incubus or Succubus
no special place to eat, no favourite colour
except they both got the blues on a regular basis.

Absolutely no pets
there was talk of a goldfish
Hades for a boy, Fugue for a girl
the upkeep and the fungus
forget that, forget birthdays
no middle names no nick names
no Casablanca, they had no song.

Mary O'Donnell

Turn, season

Stocks are pared to the core.
Truth will out. The cupboard
hoards small, silent breads.
My stomach shrinks.
At dusk, signs flow in thin jets
of flailing branch, my lover
is leaving for an unknown country.

Each day is a countdown, every leaf
hurls towards winter on the wind,
like ticking clocks I do not want to hear.
The hour will come, so the leaves say,
the quarter-hour and minute,
even the second will come when the sky
falls through bare branches.

Then my shoulders will sink
beneath the weight of a dying part,
I will hide my face,
lie low like an animal.
Cupboard doors fly unhinged,
release the staleness of borrowed days.
In the market place,

women barter for the past's
clear forms. I pass by, find shapes
set aside in the bustling space,
hand over my coins
to buy what is priceless:
new breads for the stomach,
an astute lover for the soul,

a sabre tooth for the bite of death.

Jan Conn

Near the Solimões River, 1880

What would *you* do, she asked if you came upon a man wearing
eight black-necked red *cotingas* around his waist? Their heads and
tails scarlet. Everything else glossy, buffed black. A bar tips the tail
like a blackout over the eyes of torture victims in police photographs.

As he walks towards me on his chest a snail shell and an animal
bone rub together, produce a strange arhythmic sound. The feathers
brush against me first, then other things. Birds' feet, claws clenched.

Note: There are several species of *cotinga* (Family Cotingidae); this one is *Phoenicircus
nigricollis*, Neo-tropical in distribution. The birds (above) are on a string. Collected in
1880, this Tikuna body ornament currently resides in Museum für Völkerkunde, Vienna.

Bowl and Spear

She is handed a charred wooden bowl in the form of a double-
headed jaguar. It bares its teeth. Then a spear, turquoise-feathered –
an auspicious colour. Damaged on the boat trip to Europe from the
Upper Rio Negro (1830).

She is not a warrior, she claims. (A noted delay tactic). *What then,*
they query, hiding her notebook under a tree. *Tukano, volcano,* she
murmurs as if an offering. *Heat it up. Ask for crimson.* Put on the
armadillo mask, dash off into the forest.

Note: Tukano spear, collected circa 1830. Museum für Völkerkunde, Vienna.

Arturo Carrera

Frogs

In the invisible certainty of the one who thinks these frogs
in the summer evening.

They are frogs, unlike Aesop's, that
never asked for a king log.
They are the frogs of Pringles – the most easily frightened!
The most eloquent!

Creatures whose vestigial music folds and amplifies
our distant laughter. The rumour of the passions
for which there is still room on this dark earth.

I just wanted you to remember that chorus,
that golden line.

That visual touch of sombre relief
taken swiftly by the sands of memory.

And remembering as the only knowing, enough already,

ennui of providence
moving from one moment to another
adhered to the voice, to the temporary energy
of the voice. So that its moderate meter resembles
our babbling,
our health.

I search for a memory with the conviction that the traces
that we do not see nor expect
are sparks off mixed fireflies.

...frogs by frogs heard.

Infinite accord with infinite forms without colours.

And the same lake,
the same light dune: the book?

The slightest displacement still unseen

persists

in the words.

                                    – Translated by Sergio Waisman

Hugh O'Donnell

Soap Opera

It's there in the President granting the peace-broker
a puff of pipe smoke

in the woman crossing the line marked *mother*
to another section

in the gardener balancing his mower
on the cemetery hill

in how an old lady remembers that it was
up there to the left after all –

clean as a shout, the son dying
days after his father in October,

Johanna the following June,
Jim, the railway man thirty years on –

and in Emily, Jason and Louise,
missing since Christmas, whose story

will lead like a scent to the door of a man
who knew their grandparents well.

David Butler

Millennium

The (s)city's face is in bandages, again;
staccato pneumatic schattering set-
-ting teeth   on   *edge.*
With the whoarding pulled away,
the thoUsand nUwest sUtures, {bad syntax},
Marks   where hasty skin-graft
has been tacked onto –
                    dead grey tissue.

They're: dusting-down heirlooms of masonry,
Bones of the Ascendancy years:
    georgianedwardianwilliamite
Like great-grandfathers drooling [*verdigris*] who,
    – sombre, quaint, faintly senile –,
are pushed to the front on special occasions
to   gape
into the camera.

They'll: stitch a city yet out of her faecures,
After the *BeztEuropeenMödelz*:
A Capital of bridges, of public spaces,
of [vague polysemic monuments].
Clear up the dregs from her waterways!
                    a bad hangover.
Cobble a new past out of anecdote!
                    for the visitor.

And then:
          Old Dublin, mongrel, stray,
tattered, gone in the teeth,
Will slink off down the backstreets and
disappear;
          Dubh linn,
Leaving her disconsolate litter to quibble
over the Family Name.

Augustus Young

Brine Breath
after Mallarmé / before Bukowski

I'm parrot sick, it's not fair, bookies won't take my bet.
I know too much, a legend in my lifetime, and yet
Being evens favourite is not my fancy. I'm leaving
Like the bird in the Bourbon ad, high on low-achieving,
That swoops down for a chaser on seafronts where froth meets sky.
So the end-of-the-season palms with salted hearts must die.

Oh! nights spent drinking tips with the tipsy stable-hands,
And days marking cards with dead-certs for punters in Grandstands.
But I have seen the dream-boat to China lift its anchor,
Beckon with the brochures to where Club Med tourists hanker.
I've bought the desert-isle mirage, being sold on the clean break,
Fooling myself that I'll be waved off by those I forsake.

Broken masts, no land in sight, voyages end in failures.
Yet still the sirens lure me in the shanties of drunk sailors.

PJ McNally

Beg-Meil

He paused at the perimeter
of their youth:
three French girls,
on the expanse of sand,
their skins aglow.

His straw hat and clothes
were comic
against the sun.

He gazed politely
out to sea,
aware of so many years
and the girls he'd known
in his youth.

Then he walked slowly
into the shade
of some old pine trees.

And he sat there
smiling.

Paul Murray

The Seagulls in the City

Bizarre
that you pursue me
this far out of the past,
                        arriving
in groups of two or three
on the wing,
                gliding
above the roof-tops,
and at all hours,
                        night and morning,
salting the air with your cries.

                    *

Useless
to pretend it could be different.
It cannot.
            For always
and almost against
my will
                something in my blood
wakens at the surprise of
your trespass,
                        something in my pulse
responds
to the strong, dream-like insistence
of your appearing.

                    *

At times it is enough
for me,
      and for the earth-bound
if your wings tilt
downward
      even a little.
For in that instant,
        as the mind
turns on its axis, and small wings
of desire
      begin to veer
back into the past,
it is as if the whole world
          were tilting
sideways into the wind.

§ Feature on Palestinian Poetry §

I would like to thank Ferial Ghazoul in Cairo for unstinting help with the compilation of the Palestinian poetry; also David Lloyd in California for his support, and Margaret Obank in London, Editor of *Banipal*, in whose magazine Zakaria Mohammed's poems first appeared. I must also thank Sarah Maguire in London for her enthusiastic support, and Sharif S Elmusa in Cairo for his contributions and advice. The generosity of their responses to my request for assistance was heartening, to say the least.

– Michael Smith

Mahoud Darwish was born in 1941 in Birwa, near Acre. Through his family's and his own experience he has suffered profoundly from the Israeli occupation of the Palestinian homelands. He has been actively involved in the cultural dimension of the PLO. His books include *Asafir Bila Ajniha* (*Wingless Birds*, 1960), *Awraq al-Zaytun* (*Olive Leaves*, 1964), *Ashiq Min Filastin* (*A lover from Palestine*, 1966, 1970), *Uhibbuki aw la Uhibbuki* (*I love you, I love you not*, 1972), *Qasida Bayrut* (*Ode to Beirut*, 1982) and *Madih al-Zill ali-Ali* (*A Eulogy for the Tall Shadow*, 1982). As a poet, Darwish is *both* deeply personal and political. His personal love poems fuse with the political in the most extraordinary way: it is as if the aisling ('beautiful maiden') of Jacobean Irish poetry – symbolising Ireland – became, as did not happen in Irish, a carnate, real woman. Darwish is probably the most distinguished living Palestinian poet, known throughout the Arab world as 'the poet of Palestinian resistance'.

from **A State of Siege**

Here, on the slopes of hills,
watching sunsets,
facing the cannons of time,
here by orchards with severed shadows,
we do what prisoners,
what the unemployed do:
we nurse hope.

This siege will last until we teach our enemy
selections of pre-Islamic poetry.

Pain is:
when the housewife doesn't set up the clothesline
in the morning and preoccupies herself with the cleanness of
the flag.

The soldiers gauge the distance between being and nothingness
with a tank's telescope.

We gauge the distance between our bodies and shells
with the sixth sense.

You who stand on our doorstep, come in
and drink with us Arabic coffee
(you might feel you are humans like us).
You who stand on our doorstep
get out of our mornings
so we can be certain
we are humans like you.

Behind the soldiers,
the pine trees and minarets
keep the sky from arching downward.
Behind the iron fence soldiers pee –
guarded by tanks –
and this autumn day keeps up its golden stroll
in a street wide as a church after Sunday prayer.

A humorous writer once said to me:
"If I knew the end, from the beginning,
I would have no business with words."

The siege will last until those who lay the siege feel,
like the besieged, that boredom is a human attribute.

To resist means to maintain the soundness
of the heart and testicles and your interminable disease:
hope.

Writing is a puppy biting the void;
it wounds without blood.

Our coffee cups, the birds
and green trees with blue shade,
and sun leaping from wall
toward another wall, like a gazelle,
and water in clouds of endless forms
spread across whatever ration of sky is left for us,
and things whose remembrance is deferred
and this morning, strong and luminous –
all beckon we are guests of eternity.

–Translated by Sharif S Elmusa

Fadwa Tuqan was born in 1917. She was educated at home and initiated into poetry by her brother, Ibrahim Tuqan, the well-known Palestinian poet. She has published several collections of poetry and an autobiography, *A Mountain Journey*, which has been translated into English.

To Christ the Lord on His Birthday

> *But those husbandmen said among themselves, This is the heir;*
> *come let us kill him, and the inheritance shall be ours. And they*
> *took him, and killed him, and cast him out of the vineyard.*
>
> St. Mark's Gospel XII: 7-8

O Lord, O glory of the universe,
crucified this year on your birthday,
are the joys of Jerusalem
silenced on your birthday?
O Lord, all the bells
for two millennia have not been silenced
on your birthday
except for this year:
the domes of the bells are in mourning,
black wrapped in black.

*

Jerusalem along the *Via Dolorosa*,
whipped under the cross of ordeal,
bleeding at the hands of the executioner,
and the world is a sealed heart
in the face of affliction.
In this hard indifferent world, O Lord,
the sun's eye is smothered: the world went astray
                              and was lost.
In the ordeal it did not even raise a candle.
It did not even shed a tear
to wash away the sorrows in Jerusalem.

*

The husbandmen killed the heir, O Lord,
              and raped the vineyard.
The sinners of the world fledged the bird of evil
dashing off to defile the purity of Jerusalem,
damned and infernal, hated even by Satan.

                    *

O Lord, O glory of Jerusalem,
from the well of sorrows, from the abyss,
from the depth of the night,
from the heart of plight,
the wails of Jerusalem are raised up to you.
In your mercy, take away from me, O Lord, this cup!

                              – Translated by Ferial Ghazoul

Mourid Barghouti was born in 1944 and studied English Literature at Cairo University. He has lived in the diaspora, moving from one Arab country to another, and has also spent several years in Budapest (where this poem was written). He is the author of several collections of poetry and more recently a moving memoir translated into English by Ahdaf Soueif, *I Saw Ramallah.*

Snow Poem

The horizon: a blazing colour fleeing the dictionary.
The hills have their swaying smoky blue.
No hand has painted its like.
The clouds have the colour of thousands of melted rings and
bracelets
shimmering and fleeing from their first forms:
this is a cloud of spirit, *that* of flesh.
Asphalt streets have their dark taints.
The balconies glow with their flaming roses,
The forests with their green, yellow and that orange
woven with rays, when the hand of the wind passes by the
twigs.
The bronze on the ancient domes has
turquoise progeny from centuries of rain.
On the roof tiles the dried apricot slants
on the extended pathways.
Grannies' coats take on the colour of chestnuts.
You departed when autumn was beckoning,
calling the sky with 'kerchief's tips:
'Bring your snows and sprinkle them on the city.'
But the city was not mine; I felt the chill.
Snow-flakes like birds continued
to peck eagerly at the colours
leaving over them the settled white of solitude and desolation
as if the city's colours were a thousand luminous fountains in
the dark.
Then the world stretched a hand to cut the electric cord
while you… far away…
Distance has overcome you
in a country that provokes our love and sorrow.
From a distance we approach its interiors

and enter; it distances us and moves away.
I was overcome by all the maps
in a country that witnessed my wreckage before my naming,
dispersed in exiles. Whenever I set a tent
the wind blows it away and uproots the pole.
You departed... snow in the city
but the city was not mine.
I felt the chill, as if I were the earth's only one,
and my soul, alone, burns in the snow.
You have tired me, O circular years in this alien country.
You have tired me, O circling key in a door leading to no one.

– Translated by Ferial Ghazoul

Sharif S Elmusa , a widely-published poet, scholar and translator, was born in the village of al-Abbasiyya, Palestine. He has co-edited and contributed to the anthology *Grape Leaves: A Century of Arab-American Poetry,* first published by Utah University Press in 1988, republished in 1999 in paper-back edition by Interlink Books. At present he is an Associate Professor of Political Science and Director of Middle East Studies Programme at the American University of Cairo.

Homeward Bound

Dozing off on the train late in the evening,
I miss my stop. I am tired
and can hardly walk up the stairs
to the opposite side.
I think of the old man telling me
how he used to walk for three or four hours
in the field, then hold the calves of his legs
and ask each of them if it could do more.
My legs feel his legs as they climb.

I loiter around the gray platform.
A man inspects a cigarette butt
with almost admiring attitude
then crushes it gently under his shoe.
A man and a woman talk of going
on a long journey south, perhaps inspired
by the full desert moon.
In this station faraway from downtown
there are no astonished statues
of Ancient Egyptians
reminding you how it is all out of joint.

Trying to lean against a wall
I see a file of ants running fiercely
up and down along a crack in the cement.
The ones crawling down haul tiny pieces
of straw; the ones ascending aim for the store.
Their dark bodies, shiny under a strong light,
touch on the run. None lingers or strays.
What drives them, patience or hope?
Don't their legs balk?

The body pokes the meddling mind
to mind its own business. It pricks up
its ears to listen for the sweet rumble
of the train. It craves the wide bed,
and the absent woman
to crawl beside.

– Translated by Sharif S Elmusa

Jabra Ibrahim Jabra was born in 1920. He studied in Jerusalem and at Cambridge University, majoring in English literature. He settled in Iraq after 1948 and died there in 1994. He was a prolific novelist, short story writer, poet, painter, critic and translator. The first volume of his autobiography, *The First Well: A Bethlehem Boyhood*, has been translated into English.

Love's Kingdom

The fragrance from my land
fills my chest,
evoking bygone passions
and an ever-present passion.
There I see them on the cobbled sidewalks
arguing and shouting
beneath the arches of old houses
among greengrocers and leather peddlers
among porters and donkey owners
on the edge of the dale
where we played among thorns and daisies.
They sing weep laugh and dance
displaying their staves and daggers –
theirs are iron-encrusted staves
and glittering scimitars.
The shoemaker sings for a sun
emerging like a lover from his portal,
the awl flashes in his hands like hope:
he moves it from morning to morning.
Like shepherds after their sheep slumber
the lads tell stories
awaiting a miracle
hoping the loaf of bread will suffice for
ten hungry mouths
and the fish anticipates a banquet.

Then came the years of famine:
ten loaves of bread did not suffice
for one mouth,
only laughing and singing
through a bloody grin.

From morning to morning, O my beloved,
the hours drip sounds
all black
the sun brings forth,
a bitter stinging gloom.

My first land, my paradise,
I dreamt of it in the forenoon, in the midday,
at all hours of the night.
In sorrow's kingdom
dream is the daring knight:
he is the penetrating voice
through fences of silence;
he comes and goes, then returns
to inspect the desire he disseminated,
shimmering like silver jewellery
– pendants, necklaces and bracelets –
removed by a lover's hand
and thrown on the bed
near a face, radiant like the sun.
Dream is the daring knight
in sorrow's kingdom, in terror's kingdom
and in all the kingdoms of love.

My land's fragrance
penetrates awareness,
awakening old passions,
pouncing like the perfume of a once beloved woman
left on my palms after departing —
a whiff of her hair.
Whenever the fragrance calls on me, unaware
I recall the taste of bliss on her lips.
In the land: song's scent,
hymns from oblivion,
are triggered like genies from bottles.

[. . . .]

O my beloved, with magnificent hair and temples,
can't you see, heat has come
and gone
but oppression, like sorrow, is endless.
I heard voices clamouring
in black throats around me
but my ear is on the Rock listening
to sounds coming
from a distance like cavalry's hooves
from the bottom of the rocks –
suddenly your hair flows over my face.
Your perfume fills my chest.
What have you wrapped my silence with,
love or wine?
Death-in-life or life-in-death?
How can I calm your love, O my land,
how can I respond,
O wound harrowing in my body like passionate love?

– Translated by Ferial Ghazoul

Zakaria Mohammed was born in 1951 near Nablus. He studied Arabic literature in Baghdad University. As well as poetry collections he has published a novel and a collection of plays. He lives in Ramallah and is a member of the board of directors of the Sakakini Cultural Centre.

Sun Stroke

We were born of a sun stroke
of the stroke of scythe against wind
and of horn against stone

We threw the placenta to the dogs
and our soul into a pool of gloom

Like poor women we embroidered
our lips on the fabric of silence

Impure we went to the dawn prayer
to the flower garden
and memories of childhood

Sand is our grain
and sand is the horse's fodder

We climbed the sand gasping for breath
and worn out we came down

No evidence of our names
except an alphabet not cited in the dictionary
no evidence of our forbears
except the silence of dogs at the door

We got hitched to our shoelaces
and to the hair of eyelashes
and to the tails of comets

We crouched like dogs before the door
crouched cheerless before the flower

And the flower is the blood sacrifice of midday

Our flour was strewn everywhere
and despair felt like iron in our finger tips

Grant us respite so we may recognize our shadows
and our hooves may grow

A giant bell hangs over our head
a persistent bell makes us lose the way

We pray to silence the great chime on the lips of our dead

Take us by the hand
and the waist
hold us below our breasts
we are kin of dust and fire

This is our finger
wet to explore the wind
wounded by our endless questions

We fooled around with our names
and the nakedness of shirt buttons
and drove prayers like pigs in front of us

We hitched the donkeys to children's ankles
and hitched autumn to summer
to calm down our shivers

Call us from behind our rooms
call us with a scandalous voice that would shame us bare
call us with a voice that would rip apart wood and bamboo

Lead our prayers so we may pray beyond the bound of duty
and our souls stand erect within our bodies

Bitter is our lunch
our dinner is as dry as stone
and silence flows like menstrual blood between our legs

We pray to crush our kidney stones
and pray to break the bread of our supper

No immunity for the pebble
or the rose –
all lie within the range of thunder

We were born of the inversion of the lip
and the eyelash
we were born of the stroke of horn against stone.

A House

A house
so the olive oil may flow
and candlelight flicker
and between the cracks the soul grows
and in the discord thrive the bonds
of fathers and sons

A house
so through the windows may peer
the thorn bush of the foe
a low house
so we are only a step away from the tombs of the dead

A house
for silence to fall.

– Translations by Sharif S Elmusa

Zakaria Mohammed

The Reapers

– Who are you, trekking along rough roads,
sweat secreting from your bodies?
– We are the reapers of the rolling hills.
We set out at dawn
and harvested the wind
and time
and hallucinations sprouting
like the grasses of the savanna.

O! how weird our harvest can be.
If the night hadn't fallen so soon
we would've reaped with our scythes
silence, death and stone
and descended toward the sea
and gathered the waves and their quavering
to make everything perfect,
perfect and definite.

– Translated by Sharif S Elmusa

Ghassan Zaqtan was born in 1954 in Beit Jala, near Bethlehem. He lived in Amman from 1967 to 1979 where he obtained a teacher's training degree. He has published several collections of poetry, a novel and made two documentary films. He is editor-in-chief of the quarterly *al-Shua'ra*, published by the House of Poetry in Ramallah, where he lives.

The Road in Darkness

They cry out –
but it's a night too dark to see
a hand pointing southwards

to a land sunk in shadow,
to a procession of white shrouds,
to a road of blue prayer mats…

Father, father, wake up your sons!
Stop leaning out the window!
Shake off your sadness!

Look –
at last you can walk through
a land ripe with summer!

Wake up your sons!
let them fly through this dream
as a tambourine strikes at ten on the dot

Then watch
as we slink from our caves in the hills –
a pack of lean wolves

– translated by Sarah Maguire with Kate Daniels

Ghassan Zaqtan

Four Sisters from Zakariya

Four sisters climb the mountain,
alone,
dressed in black

Four sisters
sigh
in front of the forest

Four sisters
are reading
tear-stained mail

– A train shunted through
the picture
of the settlement of Artov

– A horse
carried a girl
from our village, Zakariya

The horse whinnied
as it stood on the hill
behind the plain

Clouds
drifted lazily
over the ditch

Four sisters from Zakariya
are stood on the hill,
alone, dressed in black

– translated by Sarah Maguire with Kate Daniels

Ghassan Zaqtan

Beirut, August 1982

How I wish he had not died
in last Wednesday's raid
as he strolled through Nazlat al-Bir –
my friend with blond hair,
as blond as a native of the wetlands of Iraq.

Like a woman held spellbound at her loom,
all summer long the war was weaving its warp and weft.
And that song, *O Beiruuuuut!*,
sang from every single radio
in my father's house in Al-Karama –

and probably in our old house in Beit Jala
(which, whenever I try to find it in the maze of the camp,
refuses to be found).
That song sang of what we knew –
it sang of our streets, narrow and neglected,

our people cheek by jowl in the slums made by war.
But the song did not sing about that summer in Beirut,
it did not tell us what was coming –
aeroplanes, bombardment, annihilation…

The song was singing while my friend from Iraq –
who'd thought I was Moroccan from the countryside there –
limped bleeding to his death…
His blond hair will never fade,
a beam of light seared into memory.

– translated by Sarah Maguire with Kate Daniels

§ End of Feature on Palestinian Poetry §

Marianne Hennessy

Airport After Hours

Winner of Category B (Senior Schools) in the *SeaCat National
Poetry Competition 2002 in association with Poetry Ireland*

We were brought in through the hard, black wind
On a giant white bird.
The wheels gripped the earth and
Dragged us slowly into harbour.

Its wrought-iron wings had done their job now,
And the chirpy pilot praised its
Loyalty over the intercom.
But we were all half asleep.

The exhausted flight crew, caked in prettiness,
Quickly ushered us off with smiles and disappeared,
But we found our way
Alone through the empty airport.

An abyss of right angles and plastic tiles
Paved our way to the baggage reclaim.
Empty conveyor belts from old flights of past hours
Were still moving in their timeless ritual.

Nearby, a silver stairway escalated to nowhere.
Its passengers were long gone,
Leaving the escalator to carry only the empty air
And its own weight.

We snatched a luggage trolley and moved on to Customs,
Following the crowd until we emerged
Abruptly at arrivals
To a handful of smiling strangers.

The exit was clearly marked,
Surrounded on each side by ornamental trees.
Their reaching branches had been pruned back to reflect
The modern feel of their chrome-covered planters.

Finally, the automatic doors egested us out into
The cold, black wind,
Leaving us to fend for ourselves,
Or at least find the car.

Time to go home.
It was a long time coming.

Manus Joseph McManus

Snow

Runner-up in Category A (Adult) in the *SeaCat National Poetry Competition 2002 in association with Poetry Ireland*

Snowflakes were leaves
from the tree of heaven
whose trunk rose somewhere
between here and the Barents Sea.

They piled up to let us know
how things were in heaven,
and disappeared to show us
how it was on earth.

Desolate as geometry on paper
in a February classroom, accidental
as house-numbers, we were
each of us quite unique.

On Sundays we went to Mass;
the candles that we lit blessed us
and died, while we continued
our inimitable flickering.

Michael Clement

My Father Loved Pigeons

Runner-up in Category A (Adult) in the *SeaCat National Poetry Competition 2002 in association with Poetry Ireland*

My Father loved pigeons.
He kept them and bred them
Ever since he was a child.

He built his own cages
From wooden packing cases,
black creosote poles
And silver wire mesh.

We always had a pigeon loft in our garden.
My father would spend hours
sitting in a chair, smoking
and looking at his pigeons.

Then one day
He gave away all his precious pigeons
Until he was the only pigeon left all alone.

He dismantled his loft
Dismembering plank and pole and wire.

Then he perched upon an apartment roof
And launched himself into wingless flight.

Weary from too much flying
He fixed his navigating heart
upon the guiding stars
and let instinct and gravity
take him home.

Celia de Fréine

Grace

Runner-up in Category A (Adult) in the *SeaCat National Poetry Competition 2002 in association with Poetry Ireland*

Tá Grace Paley tagtha chun na tíre seo
agus táim féin is scata cairde cruinnithe
i gColáiste na Trionóide le héisteacht léi.

Oíche ar an mbaile. Sos ó dhíospóireachtaí Dála
is ó ghuth cosantach an Aire Sláinte.
Ní air atá an locht go bhfuil bean ag fáil bháis

in ospidéal sa chathair. Ach cé atá á deifriú
chun a huaighe? Cé atá ag iarraidh uirthi foirm
a shaighneáil is glacadh le cuid an bheagáin?

Tá a dáréag gasúr cruinnithe thart uirthi
gasúir a bhfuil a gcéimeanna ceiliúrtha aici –
na chéad fhiacla, na chéad fhocail.

Tá a fhios aici nach scuabfaidh sí an clúmhach
dá ngúnaí céime amach anseo
nach gcuideoidh sí leo a *trousseaus* a cheannach

nach slíocfaidh sí síoda róbaí baiste a garpháisti.
Is mian léi go dtuigfidh a gasúir
nach ise atá ciontach in aon pháirt de seo.

Tá a fhios ag an dáréag cruinnithe thart ar a leaba
nach gcloisfidh said gáir mholta uaithi
an lá a mbronnfar céimeanna orthu

nach mbeidh sí ansin le barróg a bhreith orthu
lá a bpósta, nach bhfeicfidh sí
a loirg ar cheannaithe a ngasúirse.

Déanaim iarracht m'intinn a dhiriú ar bhlas Grace Paley
blas a aithním ó chaint Sipowicz is Simone,
faoistiní á dtarraingt acu as a gcoirpigh.

Ach ní leor mo smaointe ar Sipowicz is Simone
nó scéalta siopaí mangarae Nua Eabhrach
nó comharsanachta Íudacha

chun m'aird a tharraingt ó bheathaí ghasúir na mná seo
mar a bheidh said is mar ba chóir dóibh a bheith.
Feicim ina leaba í, feicim í á haerscuabadh

ó ghrianghraif an albaim theaghlaigh
Leanann blas Nua Eabhrach air. Leannann duine
des na banscríbhneoirí is suimiúla ar domhan

is ní féidir liom ach smaoineamh
ar dhuine des na mná is misniúla ar domhan
atá ag fáil bháis in ospidéal sa chathair
agus ar an Aire atá á deifriú chun a huaighe.

An English translation of this poem, by the author, is available on the Internet at
www.irishpoetry2002.com/adult_2002.html

Michael Coady

Thirteen Souls with Bread and Wine

Runner-up in Category A (Adult) in the *SeaCat National Poetry
Competition 2002 in association with Poetry Ireland*

The blind man
behind the pillar.

The bent woman
on two sticks.

The man with two pens
and a stone
in his pocket.

The bad singer
who always sings.

The dancer
who may have to have
her breast removed.

The priest whose mind
is elsewhere.

The mother who always brings
a Christmas dinner
to the cemetery.

The man who hooked
and lost the only
salmon of his life.

The nun who is beginning
to forget the days.

The man who plays
bass drum in the band.

The woman who paints
her toenails red
in summer.

The sergeant who overcame
the demon.

The baker's wife
lighting one candle
from another.

John O'Donnell

The Majestic

Winner of Category A (Adult) in the *SeaCat National Poetry Competition 2002 in association with Poetry Ireland*

For This Week Only warned the message
in black marker on the latest glossy poster, as we
queued at The Majestic all those rain-filled afternoons
in the summer we discovered sex, and the ravages

of acne. More than the roar and flicker of the screen,
what mattered was what was happening here: wolf-whistles,
the footstamping and cheers from StarCrushed mouths as lights
went down, and we sat through the ads, the jerky newsreel,

Forthcoming Attractions on first dates, row on row
of one-armed crucifixions waiting for the action
to begin. High up, Fitzy – balding, tipsy – knocked back
one more shot as he loaded the projector and shambled down

to stand beside the swing-doors watching over us, a Zeus
in platform shoes. Cloud-eyed, we thanked God for the rain
skittering on streets as we turned, wet-lipped and full of purpose,
to each other amid the susurrus of sweet wrappings, urgent

fumblings in the mote-filled dark. We were young and scared
of nothing except heartbreak, the lasso of Fitzy's flashlight
twirling all around us as we struggled with zips and buttons,
groping towards the future with trembling clammy hands.

Mary O'Donnell

Poetry in Crisis?
[A response to Michael Smith's editorial essay, 'Poetics and Related Matters', *Poetry Ireland Review* 73.]

Language, grasped as a system, goes dumb (Elias Canetti, 1969)

That poetry as an art 'is in crisis' is a statement which surfaces every so often among poets, not unlike the lament of those who every so often inform the world that 'the novel is dead.' Neither statement, it seems to me, has the slightest grounding in the realities of either art. But the feeling of working within a crisis-ridden genre is overwhelmingly strong for many artists, who – finding themselves regularly confronted by the perception that written art must be at least entertaining and certainly immediately accessible to listening audiences – can hardly be blamed if a note of panic creeps into the ongoing poet-to-poet dialectic.

We need to reflect a little on both historical hinterlands and contemporary foregrounds to understand the notion of a 'crisis' in what is essentially an aesthetic concern. There seems no question about the fact that many poets have traditionally oscillated between the feeling that the genre was inadequately heard, being undermined by the activities of fellow practitioners, and the occasional glory-moment in which the world briefly, glowingly, responded to what they (and others who think just like them) were saying. I have a distinct empathy for this poet-in-isolation, working with consciousness and language, for the man or woman chipping away on bits of paper, probing the phenomenal boundaries which reject or discard the noumenal, *das Ding an sich* – that which haunts archetypal poets and pushes them to reject the system, and whatever word-shapes and mouth-utterances are systemic, position-oriented or Prozac-logical. These are the poets in crisis, for sure. These – our fellow creatures clad in the skin of a human, placed firmly within a social system which rewards position, affluence, glamour, material endurance, chick-lit and 'irreverent/funny' doggerel – are living in an interior far North, the equivalent of the literary salt-mines for which they sense little respect.

They may be crisis-ridden due to over-exposure to barbarian values, but poetry is not, per se, in crisis, no more than hitherto in literary history, the point being that most of us – marooned in the contexts of the present – experience at some time or other the sensation of being at the pinnacle of some variously defined idea of progress, a sensation which is in fact quite illusory.

That the sense of crisis continues is all to the good, and the idea of good poets writing at odds with the world is nothing new. How else can good poets write? To be a poet in the first place is to have said goodbye to any flirtation with 'position' (in the socially accepted sense of that word), with what the majority-approved view of anything is; it is like giving a jubilant two fingers to the notion that a) we are all part of the same group who b) share mostly the same political, social, economic and liberal whey-faced views on most information-based subjects.[1]

Poets themselves exist within a social and economic system which wordlessly conveys the view that most mysteries, even the poetic, runic ones, can be decoded if you find the right formula. Poetry then, according to this outlook, is something simply thrown down on paper with the flamboyance of a visual artist thrashing paint around the canvas and then cycling across it (which isn't to denigrate that technique either, but to make the point that the potential audience for either poetry or painting sometimes seems convinced that the self-referential, unlettered 'abstract' is enough, that anything goes, that it is sufficient to pronounce the produced poem – or painting – as something that 'just happened', a bit like unplanned sex). However, the difference between the poem that 'just happened' in a self-indulgent splurge of faulty – if fashionably colloquial – syntax and lego-like construction, and unplanned sex is that the former has no point of reference outside the self. It is a static, frigid form, devoid of the capacity to make the essential connection with something beyond the self, it cannot move outside the accepted phenomenal. The result of this is that the relationship with 'meaning' is absent, and also the idea of a metaphysical journey integral to the construction of a work of aesthetic incandescence.[2] Again, a bit like sex, with roots in the repetitious deep-space of collective history, art compulsively attempts to re-invent the congruent delights of earthly and spiritual knowledge, over and over again.

The current crisis for me is based on what I regard as the 'dumbing down' of work which has to be read more than once in order to be understood. No matter how poets evaluate the meaning of what they are about (and most poets think a lot about the source of their art and how it might flow), when it comes to the question of poetry readings, the reality for many is that there is little place for the poet who is not a 'crowd-puller.' The 'bums on seats' syndrome so beloved of the world of theatre has entered the poetry arena, and in many of our stunningly-designed, well-funded new arts centres replete with state-of-the-art lighting and sound systems, arts administrators nationwide are under pressure to fill those auditoriums in a time of mounting cutbacks. I cannot blame them. The integrity of performance, visual, musical and written art is contingent on an integrity of *belief* in the experimental nature of those same arts.

Nor am I certain if there is actually one, single group at which the finger can be pointed. Poets must simply, it seems to me, come to terms with the fact that the Irish public does not greatly care for poetry, despite all the reverential mouthings about the subject among people who should ideally have a feel for the subject (English teachers, and lay-people who consider themselves to be 'readers'). The 'readers' in our society do not actually read much poetry, although they might be aware of who has published what. Yet 'readers' who do not actually read the contemporary are amazingly authoritative on it nonetheless and often quite at home with the notion that poetry should be 'immediate' and 'accessible'. Some poets are equally comfortable with immediacy and accessibility too and I have no cavil with such poetry so long as there is a respected space available for the poetry which has a totally different axis. I am speaking about poetry which collects the silences between the babble of what is acceptable, I am speaking about poetry which does not compromise for the sake of pleasing others, I am speaking about poetry which is prepared to put limbs into the sewers of human experience, which is capable of shrinking to the gravitational density of an object in a black hole, and which unremittingly does not care whether or not anyone is pleased.

This is not to be confused with my earlier comments on the self-referential. The poet who refuses to pander to the entertainment brigade, who refuses to play court-jester in the world of language, is in fact the diametrical opposite of the sentimentalist or humorist. This poet feels no pressure to be amusing, and has long ago decided that poetry – although quirky and wry at times – is generally much more connected to an authentic examination of consciousness than it is to comedy, and feels no need to accommodate the contemporary zeitgeist in its diluted forms. Neither are there many others, if you're playing the numbers game, for whom to write. Some poets recognise this. It does not matter. Other poets sometimes read the work, plus a thin shaving of readers who are not poets. The rest, you realise as time goes on, are completely and utterly connected to fitting in an hour at a health and leisure centre, meeting for a pizza after Thursday late-night shopping, speaking energetically on such subjects as housing costs, interior design, labels on clothes and that poisonous social species known as the *mobile phone*. These are the contemporary passions, whether poets like it or not. That is what we must live with. In other centuries there was something else to come to terms with, perhaps illiteracy, lack of access, the seriousness of contagious disease, the undemocratic structure of education.

We as poets are inheriting the best and the worst aspects of the democratisation of our culture. We are cohabitators with other specialists on life's suburban plain, trained to the notion of individuality and uniqueness, to various buzz-words that make people feel better about themselves, and an accompanying awareness that as poets we live like monks in the flurry of the demotic, yet are casually regarded as *equal specialists* (you have your poetry, I have my photography) when we believe deeply, profoundly, that poetry is not about and never has been about equalities of any kind. That, and only that, is the true locus of the crisis in art.

While there is *access* now, insofar as anyone can travel a short distance today and find themselves a poetry reading, for example, there is also a peculiar inability (or unwillingness) to actually absorb what poets are saying and (more significantly) doing. The mind apparently blocks such concepts. The majority can read today, unlike one hundred and fifty years ago, yet the majority has never seemed less inclined to examine the humming dialectic between writer, nature and existence which is laid bare in the best poetry. Furthermore most people believe themselves to be conceptually equipped to critique what they are reading, and mistakenly believe that relative literacy plus a sprinkling of critical terms often purloined from the world of the movie-buff equips them with the ability to decide who is 'good' and who is not. This, in turn, filters into the world of poetry, I believe, fostering petty rivalries. Yet *some* of the petty rivalries are themselves tolerable, because one realises that they are merely the response of one wave of poets to another, usually older one. The established voices are there to be challenged, and the Young Turks arrive every ten years or so, hell-bent on upending whatever and whoever preceded them. It is a natural agitation between poets, and we should welcome it, *because without a competitive agitation of the creative kind, poetry stagnates.*

Like a great deal else in our culture, poetry too has skipped a stage in its development. Just as the economic line shot sharply to the top of the graph from the early nineties on in a development for which few were prepared and to which we are still adjusting, so too with poetry. Yes, we may have by-passed 20th century modernism, or a lot of it, leap-frogging gaily over the shoulders of the elders[3] to arrive at something resembling post-modernism, but that may not matter if we are not complacent, if we do not assume that poetry is a sort of pseudo-mystical writing-by-numbers game, or that there are self-advancement codes to be cracked and 'How To' books to be absorbed if one wants to head to the top of the poetry class.

Elias Canetti was referring to a 'social' system when he spoke of language being rendered dumb. That is the enemy: finding our energies, marshalling whatever it takes to be poets, just to be poets[4] and not think of audience laughter at our witty outpourings, nor to think of sales figures (for the majority, modest!) or putting the spin on our 'themes' to make them palatable enough for a mid-morning radio programme or television. Not all poets are smiling, dimpled creatures. Not all poets invest in charm. Not all have the *mot juste* to hand when it comes to conveying what their poetic fixation, their existential preoccupations and compulsions, are actually about.

If anything, this is a truly challenging time to be writing poetry. Never has anti-intellectualism been at such an all-time high, combined with such gross confidence and scant humility. In the nineteen-eighties we used to hear stories of football stadiums being filled to capacity for poetry readings in the Eastern Bloc countries. How we envied that capacity to ensnare a public in such need of the ironic and subversive! Now, people clearly do understand the language and moods of the subversive – at least the concept is understood, judging by contempo-rary advertising on television – but it is despised, relegated to the bunkers of what is seen as no longer necessary and has no possible purpose, beyond immediate humour for those-in-the-know.

To survive the overweaning arrogance of the in-joke culture is part of the problem and part of the challenge for today's poets. The poetry is fine, and will be. So are most of the poets, if they can hold out and just write. And not be too willing to please.

[1] To be informed is sometimes the not-so-subtle enemy of 'to know': Henri Bergson has much to say about the vital, active, principle of knowledge that exists in everybody.

[2] Take, for example, one poem which moves fluidly on the surface and has a narrative flow, *but also, significantly,* having a lot to say – with urgency – is attempting and achieving something much greater than the sum of its formal and accessible parts, Paul Durcan's *A Snail in My Prime.*

[3] Sometimes lazily, believing the stereotype that because we were Irish we were good, regardless of what we wrote.

[4] The Greek poet Pindar once said that our chief duty consists in *becoming who we are...*

Maurice Harmon

The Era of Disappointment

Pat Boran, *As the Hand, the Glove*, Dedalus, 2001, pb. €8.80.
Gregory O'Donoghue, *Making Tracks*, Dedalus, 2001, pb. €8.80.
Paddy Bushe, *Hopkins on Skellig Michael*, Dedalus, 2001, pb. €8.80.
Moyra Donaldson, *Beneath the Ice*, Lagan Press, 2001, pb. £6.95.
Peter Carpenter, *The Black-Out Book*, Arc Publications, 2002, pb. £4.95.

In contemporary Irish poetry the elegiac mood is pervasive. At least three of these collections have a more than usual concentration on the experience of death and loss. Of course, when someone close to us dies we feel the need to express grief. But apart from those particular instances, there is in Ireland now a general sense of loss, a feeling of let-down found in the language itself. It comes I suspect from the realisation that we live in an era of disappointment, when whatever hope or illusion we had about the country's liberalism, tolerance, or basic decency has been shattered by the discovery of dishonesty, hypocrisy, cynicism, and greed on a vast scale. We have been betrayed by those in positions of authority and power. We do not find salvation in an institution, or in a received body of beliefs. All we have is our imaginations and the determination to use language to express the truth we experience. Knowing that language itself is being corrupted day after day by the merchants of spin, we try to keep it pure, and see that as the primary task.

The title of Pat Boran's collection comes from the poem 'Flesh', which affirms the primacy of the living substance. In itself this is a welcome celebration and indicative of the pervasive mood of the poetry. Even poems that grieve over the death of a father, a lover or a friend, do so in the context of the vitality of life and love. 'Flesh' concludes in a language whose simplicity and directness makes the claim all the stronger:

> I say it again: the spirit loves
> the flesh as the hand, the glove.

> And if you doubt me, ask my dying father
> which he would rather:

to be done at last with love and pain,
or to leave, but then come back to flesh again.

The elegy 'For S with AIDS' places the theme of loss and mortality within the cyclical process of life and decay, growth and fall, and does so in a manner that might seem callous or opportunistic until one understands the way in which grief is transmuted. Elegies not only cry out their pain, they bring in the note of consolation – the portrait of the dead father in 'Lost and Found' for example, is deeply moving.

The poem in memory of Lar Cassidy called 'Afterlife' has an unusual directness and emotional force. To confront feeling in this way requires technical control, but Boran has his personal voice and idiom. The language, his language, works. The context is copulating flesh: a couple in the back yard, in a red Escort, with the headlights flooding the room where the speaker gets 'those few and terrible words' of his friend's death. Even here, in the philosophical spirit that guides the collection, he knows the living must accept these words 'as a new place to begin'. His first reaction is to fling something at the lovers in the car, to shout at them to '*kill the lights*', because

> *...There are souls*
> *trying to sleep (or mourn or brood)*
> *under your jerking strobes...*

In a smooth transition from a portrait of the self on 'other nights', he moves from irritation to a more measured reflection on mortality and the community of death we all become part of 'when the lights go out'. Maybe it is right, he thinks, addressing the dead man...

> you should be rising up
> on this twin helix, carried aloft
> or on to where our wavering hope
>
> in an afterlife,
> in a better life and love
> and place than this,
> will be, if there is a god, absolved.

That the lights of the car become the twin helix may seem too daring, but the tone carries the idea of elegy's traditional transmutation of the dead to a better place. Boran also has an amused and ironic intelligence that sees the possibilities for comedy in Cosimo Rosselli's 'Virgin and Child Enthroned with Saints', Edward Hopper's filling station, or being ill in New York. His poems are flexible enough to lift off the page.

Although Gregory O'Donoghue's poems lack that lightness of spirit, they have their own momentum. He has a reflective sensibility that sometimes broods over experience, remembering and recording in a serious tone, as in the elegy 'Ropes of Sand'. The 'I' persona is present in a funeral home, 'seeing everything', including the marks of death, and appreciating that the remains have not been made pretty with cosmetics.

O'Donoghue, in this poem, comes at his friend indirectly and without trying to transmute the experience. With but a slight shift to brief evocation of the beauty of place, he remembers their camping together in their 'hobo hippy days.' He pays tribute:

> Green knight. Born in the month of the barley
> harvest, and the flowering of the holly.
>
> Humour, pride. Yet also that brooding course
> in you deepening and bedding through
> the years until, drop by erosive drop,
>
> it could no longer excel itself, take
> a wild jump outside its own banks and sing
> at the top of the nearest living tree.

This kind of level-headed language is characteristic. The passion is in the quiet and accurate commemoration. Behind the manner and behind the brooding memory lies pain, loss and appreciation.

At the same time O'Donoghue has an eye for the beauty of the natural world, as in 'Bicycles' seen leaning as one near a wood. He imagines them going downhill and returning with an 'uphill wobble, / youngling linnet's test-flight...' It is April, and the poet observes how

...brightness falls on
the spokes of a sidelong wheel,
still turning: charm-sparkle
of webbed dew, wooing the sun.

The metaphors fall easily into place as the attentive warmth of tone
alters something quite ordinary and unimportant into something
magical, without overdoing it.

A similar happy mood runs through 'Roads' where the poet's
command of the language of trains gives life to the poem. It has at the
same time an 'unfussed regard, matter-of-fact timbre'. This is not the
manner of Stephen Spender's express; it is not trying to mimic motion
in words or to personify trains; the aim is more down-to-earth, but it
adds up, has variety – of settings, of engines and wagons – and is
quietly enjoyable and accomplished:

Only when you've cleared the sidings and curve
off the feeding road onto the fast road,
when the clatter over the points gives way

to rhythm, can you know it all might hold together.
Just about – like today's gallivanting wagons,
frisky, yet not over-light on their flanges.

And the sun is smiling too, doing a dance,
polishing the rails, everything –
hours away my three-day-leave begins:

tomorrow these wagons can kiss buffers
in ten different midnight shunting yards;
I'll go to Bottesford, see my girlfriend.

The opening poem of Paddy Bushe's collection is a kind of annuncia-
tion: a wren crashes into a window, is covered with a cloth not in the
hope of revival but as an act of kindness. But the bird recovers, flies out
the door, to explore 'pockets of light and air', to 'sway and sing in the
ruffling wind'. The poet exults in this resurrection:

My heart sang too, as if suddenly lifted
To majestic heights on an eagle's back.

There is an attractive ease of movement and development in this poem, an effective association of image, a simplicity of response to the bird's initial plight, the central theme which is carried through right from the opening line to the last.

Bushe's delight in landscape, its vistas and landmarks, is exhilarating in 'A Drive to Eyries'. As in the case of the wren the relationship between poet and subject is open and shared...

That day, that journey, there was no horizon.
Sunlight bounced off the sea like words
And mountain roads wound around themselves
Like an endless conversation with God.

Time itself swung between the huge
Stone walls of the fort at Staigue,
Ponderous with age, and the bobbing
Plastic mussel-rafts at Kilmackilloge.

'Metamorphosis' is a similar poem of accurate observation, this time of seals on 'the low-tide slabs.' Given the trust established in previous poems, one can relax here into the enjoyment of rhythm and language as the poet opens his heart and sings a song of praise to these 'Splendidly pedestalled' creatures who have 'no need / Of the huge theatricalities of light'. Again, in addition to the deft selection of images, there is that frank, uninhibited delight in what the poet observes.

A poem like 'Planting Garlic' reveals the same primordial closeness to nature we find in Patrick Kavanagh. Not that Bushe is overshadowed by him, he has his own field to plough, his own area of concentration. It is this quality of focussing that stands out. Like Liam O'Flaherty in *Spring Sowing*, the imagination seizes reality, connects with it, recreates it in vibrant language.

It is, of course, not all plain sailing, not all wonder and praise. Here too, as with Boran and O'Donoghue, the Angel of Death appears. In 'Stroke', a father suffers a stroke and Bushe records with pained honesty the slow progress towards death, the false hopes, the tiny improvements, the questions friends ask in concern, the memories of how the man 'stepped acres all over / It seemed, every country in Ireland'. 'So how / Is he now?' neighbours ask: 'Much the same, I supposed.'

But of course he is much the same as he has been since the stroke; not much the same as he once used to be. In four sections of six stanzas each Bushe sets out the sad progression that we all recognise. It is strangely moving and consoling to see grief and love addressed so calmly and accurately. This is just one of a number of laments, achingly real, lovingly honest.

The title poem in ten parts is different from the others in being dramatised and having a more austere kind of language, as it places the poet-priest on the penitential rocks of Skellig Michael. Hopkins is making a 'retreat' in the hope that the jagged place may *'edge'* him *'with brightness.'* We move into the pilgrim's mind; his reflections on the tough, isolated place have echoes from his poetry; he reads the scene in terms of his own spiritual needs, finding God's presence and seeing in the conduits that conduct water into the wells not the miracles of popular belief yet

> A miracle still, he mused, of intent,
> Of will to stay, of work, to channel
> Water through stone as grace through spirit.
> *Laborare orare est. Aqua vita est.*

Enduring a storm – its description one of the most effective sections of the poem – he finds direction in the beam from the lightness. In Section viii he looks for 'paradigms' in the death of a puffin torn by a falcon, and finds them in the etymology of peregrine and *peregrinatio*, pilgrimage for Christ, hawk and victim in Christ's sacrifice. Next morning he finds comfort in the warmth of the sun and his sense of belonging to a universal church.

There is much that is satisfying about these sections, a well-honed language that handles the progression of experience and realises what is spiritual in the description of place. The poem interfaces with Hopkins poetry in a complex and sophisticated manner.

Moyra Donaldson's poem 'Unguarded Words' comments on her state of being: self-examination and self-criticism are good for the poetic soul. The poem suggests a cleansing of excess: 'I am resolved / to buckle down'. She recognises the need for restraint, to accept the happy medium despite the 'constant hunger' that consumes her, the desire for extremes. 'The Straw', dealing with finding her lover with another woman, is humorous where it might have been pained, ironical where it might have been sentimental –

> she forgave him his trespasses,
> those she knew, and those she guessed at

even though she knows they have been making use of 'her new sofa / that she hadn't even got to sitting down on yet herself'. This is the last straw, maybe even the one that broke the camel's back. She has had enough of forgiving.

Donaldson takes romantic experience with an astringent grain of salt – 'she fell for the crooked man / and went to live with him in his little crooked house'. It is, she admits, 'a long crooked mile back'. It is not a question of once bitten, twice shy; the memory lingers on in 'Out Damned Teeth Marks'. His teeth marks on her palm are evidence of passion, and while she can sluice away the other signs and smells, this is indelible:

> ... she is slow to mend
> weeks later
> a ghost trace still remains
>
> her life's moved out of joint

'Anecdotal Words' brings the note of sadness nearer. The lovers on a Belfast Sunday have nowhere to go. His words prove nothing, he will always be hidden from her. The poem is wonderfully detailed and contextual in its depiction of the bleak city and the sense of hopeless-ness. Her honest assessment is the most positive element in the poem, as it is in Donaldson's work as a whole.

> Her words are a frozen weir
> where a woman floats, dreaming beneath the ice.

His kisses will not warm her, nothing will melt –
there will never be anything between them but regret.

Her poems are haunted by images and thoughts of age, loss, emptiness and a fragile sense of helplessness. The song of a bird singing in the night is at first a cause of delight, but when the novelty wears off their sleep is disturbed; the bird stands for something they can never reach...

Birdsong disturbs our sleep, our dreams
are filled with feathered longing as if
we too are being called by some thing
or some place we'll never reach now.

In this ending the poem goes beyond its immediate contexts towards the evocation of something beyond reality. A similar lift beyond the immediate comes in 'Daffodils', a descriptive poem about going to buy the flowers, the mother planting them, but then after she dies they are 'painfully there, like the resurrection of love'. In 'Lethe', a lament for the mother, the poet's hurt sensibility comes into view:

If only misery could be wiped away like memory
like chalk marks from a board, lessons over.

But it is not erased that easily. The poem is a poignant expression of love and of the inability of the young to help when the parent becomes terribly sick. Despite the pain at its centre the poem moves easily, keeping within its range.

Peter Carpenter in *The Black-Out Book* maintains a neutral tone: he keeps his distance, records in a quiet, unemotive manner, holds our attention precisely because his poetry is tactfully declining to make excessive demands on us, not trying too hard, as in 'Concealed Entrance', an account of a journey in Northern Ireland:

...after whitewashed
outhouses, holiday homes in Bushmills,
concealed entrances to lounge bars,
a marking of time in the wipers...

[...]

even as we eye the waves,
contemplate what it is to live
on such an island with, all the time,
this power, waiting at our leisure,

marking out its territory in foam,
tearing back into itself before
occupying the sand, again drawn
into it, again giving us pause.

Carpenter has a wary, sceptical intelligence; he is at times ironical in his contemplation, with a touch of Louis MacNeice, as in 'All Clear': 'This is London / breaking into light / appliances working the Thames / a double decker / advertising Schweppes'. He can be humorous about a mundane activity, as in 'Potato Junkers', where the peeling is made to resemble an air-raid over Stettin.

...Primary target:
any old King Edward's from the surfaces
clustering. I prong one...

[...]

...pinpoint its tuberous spires, start
to flatten vulnerable settlements
and define its centre with my blade. Hours
of it. I grow to admire it. It gives only
after silent resistance. There'll be no
tearful ringing crises: it's no onion.

No tears where none are intended, just faith in the imagination. We cannot ask more of the lyric than that it expresses the poet's situation and his or her imaginative responses to it.

James J McAuley

Five Firsts

Patrick Warner, *All Manner of Misunderstanding*, Killick Press (St. John's, Newfoundland), 2001, pb. $12.95.
Anna Wigley, *The Bird Hospital*, Gomer Press (Llandusul, Ceredigion, Wales), 2002, pb. £6.95.
Eilish Martin, *Slitting the Tongues of Jackdaws*, Summer Palace Press, 1999, pb. €11.50.
Mary Branley, *A Foot on the Tide*, Summer Palace Press, 2002, pb. €11.50.
Lisa Steppe, *When The Wheat Horses Die*, Summer Palace Press, 2001, pb. €11.50.

The small world of poetry publishing is a source of wonder for anyone with connections to it. Book publishing in general is suffering a backlash from the global economy, complicated by self-imposed restrictions in the English-language book trade, and by arcane copyright law. The five books reviewed here are from small independent publishers in Newfoundland, Wales, and Donegal, not generally thought of as meccas of literary publishing. All three presses listed here get token grant assistance, without which they would not survive for long. But the chronic problem is distribution; it is virtually impossible for the Canadian and Welsh publishers listed here to place their titles with Irish booksellers, even with those who do stock contemporary Irish poetry. A frustrating state of affairs; yet new poetry continues to be published by presses like these, and more power to them.

It would be a shame if Patrick Warner's intriguing first collection wasn't available in Ireland. This Mayo man, currently a librarian in St. John's, Newfoundland, writes thought-provoking, densely textured verse with enviable assurance, nicely poised between its colloquial diction and its taut, carefully measured lines. His subjects provide the standard fare of contemporary poetry: urban and rural scapes, personal recollection and epiphany, the act and art of writing itself. (Wallace Stevens remarked that the only subject of poetry was poetry itself.)

His originality, therefore, depends on his management of point-of-view. He makes no bones about his first-person-singular stance, but makes quirky, sneaky shifts of tone and downright changes of mind to reach conclusions. All very well, but he often left this reader blinking, astonished at how he got there from where he started.

The short poem from which the book derives its title is a fair example of his method. Here it is *in toto*:

Leviathan

A grain of sand
has made the oyster.
This irritant
has set in motion
an inward rhythm,
a worrying S&M
in the ocean's vast ear.

When she answers,
silver fishes thread
the rising waves,
sending the boatman's
heart-a-fluttering,
giving rise to all manner
of misunderstanding.

'a worrying S&M' sets off strange trains of thought! But Mr Warner's shorter poems are not his strongest. About half of the book consists of longer poems, usually of several sections; others, like 'Bears', develop a narrative in phases rather than in chronological order. These are artfully constructed deliberations on images, while the subjects announced in the titles compel us to expand the limits of association. In 'Toggle', images from an archaeological dig combine with those of recovery from wristbone surgery; then the epiphany:

...much like the way the future is made
when the elements are coalesced by a will
that is, for a short time, sharper than stone,
harder and brighter than polished steel.

In 'Compass' he twists John Donne's notorious conceit around on his teacher's blackboard for an amusing juggled metaphysics of his own.

Indeed, his method of weaving concept with image often seems mindful of Donne, the sensuous and the rational dancing with each other in sometimes incongruous quickstep. This at any rate is one way of reading Mr. Warner's work; most poems require several readings and may reward closer scrutiny than a reviewer can always afford. Certainly, though, this is a poet of ample imagination and technical skill. (A nice design touch, by the way: the cover includes a detachable bookmark!)

While you must look closely for the crocuses in Patrick Warner's poem of that title, Anna Wigley presents her 'Crocuses' directly:

> Cold flames
> Blossoming from cold grass
> in the nettled wind.
>
> [...]
>
> their little chalices
> clean as March sunlight,
> bright as courage.

More than half the contents of this prizewinning poet's book are sharply focussed, succinctly phrased nature-poems. The remainder creates the same effect as that of opening an old album – portrait-elegies, domestic interiors, a few love poems, hospital visits, etc. Her subjects, therefore, are neither original nor remarkable; but she makes them her own with an attentive sympathy and graceful, reticent language that makes each poem enlightening:

> your feet already past shame
> in the intimate slippers,
>
> the cavity of your chest
> beneath the wool, unfleshed
> like the bare stone of a fruit...
>   – 'Frank'

– and she can be sharply satirical:

its almost-single bed
a neat confession
of your bare-boarded life
and lightly furnished heart.

– 'Trace'

She has a lovely, insightful poem to Iris Murdoch, while her consistently accurate descriptions lend her work a certain durability. Succinctness of line and form places the focus almost exclusively on her patterns of diction and imagery. Her method is successful enough for occasional lapses into sentimentality to be easily forgiven.

Summer Palace Press, a comparatively new imprint based, makes an auspicious beginning with three poetry collections published over the past three years.The books are handsomely designed, with striking covers using contemporary artists, full-page authors' photos, and a clear unobtrusive typeface on generous page layouts. The Newmann's of Kilcar, Co. Donegal deserve commendation.

Eilish Martin tries out varied line-lengths with varied degrees of success, leaving the impression that she is uncertain about relation of form to content. A central poem, 'Epiphany in Bombay Street', is composed of unrhymed three-line stanzas with lines of uneven length from eighteen to five syllables. It narrates the life of an Indian door-to-door salesman in an unnamed city (Belfast?) with its colonial street-names and pious housewives. The epiphany of the title seems to be the 'death-comes-to-all' recognition of the women when 'Raja-mataz' doesn't come on his rounds any more. Ms. Martin relies almost completely on place- and brand-names and familiar Latin liturgical phrases to carry the tale, so to speak. Neither form nor detail manages to lift the poem to a level above the anecdotal, and this is regrettably the case with several of her poems.

What does sustain the reader's interest is her passionate commitment to exploring the relation of inner self to outward experience, even the mundane, which in her best poems leads to a genuine *mythopoesis*, exemplified by 'Of Earth and Air':

your shirt caught on the yellow gorse, abandoned for a loose shift
of water, your feet bedded

on pebbles the colour of pewter, your arms a hoop of shadow
nursing my head in its lap.

I suspect that if Ms. Martin placed more trust in the unifying, forming functions of rhythmical patterns, by which to effect 'increments of meaning', her poetry will do more justice to her considerable imaginative powers.

Mary Branley also has some trouble with basic techniques of versification; but – perhaps acknowledging this – she keeps things simple, with generally short lines and short poems, some of which leave you wishing she'd been a bit more expansive on her subject:

Yearning

I need the sound
of the uilleann pipes –
raw escape of pain along the veins,
squeezing of air at the elbow,
the difficulty breathing.

A native of Sligo, this poet has returned to the northwest after living abroad for some years. Even when the poems are on such topics as 'Holloway Boys' (thumbnail sketches of rascals only a teacher could love), or located in North Carolina, or the Canary Islands –

High up, we tourists
on the windy terrazzo
of the Vaca Azul
watch the sun go down
in the African sea.
                              – 'Winter Solstice

– there is a definite sense of a northwest accent, as it were, in almost every poem. One is reminded of another poet, whose simplicity of style and roots in the folk culture of his native region followed him overseas and brought him back here constantly: Padraic Colum. Ms. Branley also shares with that modest man a rare directness and generosity of spirit.

Beginning with the opening lines of Lisa Steppe's first poem, 'Ascension', we are in a radically different world, the surreal territory between actual experience and the subconscious:

> When she was a child in the bunkers
> of the last war, she used to play a game.
> She would plant a May tree in the centre
> of the air raid shelter where creatures
> crouched in darkness; where the pressure
> cooker of detonations worked on her hearing...

– and this sentence continues for eighteen more lines, across two stanza-breaks, the unrelenting psychic pressure building to its inevitable ironic release, 'back to terra firma.'

Ms. Steppe's poems are grounded in, but never settled on, *terra firma*. Their astounding effects follow Emily Dickinson's dictum, 'Tell all the Truth but tell it slant...' Her language is spare, highly concentrated; line-breaks trigger intense sparking of one image off another, the effect like that for a non-Egyptologist reading heiroglyphs: we're not sure we understand, but we certainly feel deep, meaningful patterns unfolding:

> His predator's skin
> is oxenhide, fresh from the tanner.
> The outer layer, slick and suave.
>
> I wonder whether we sweethearts,
> creatures of ragout fin
> and pie, really love that guy?
>
> Or is it Daddy we try
> to placate, trading a kiss
> for the rapids, the falls.
>
> – 'Cantos di Luz y Amor'

If we simply connect the imagery, and allow their connotations full play; accept the strange stasis of fragmented or discombobulated syntax that compels us into irrationality and synthesis; cross over time-lapsed, disjointed chronologies...then we can begin to pick up hints and glimpses of the central subject:

> Last Sunday I dived to the bottom
> Of Lough Cronagorma. Gently but skilfully
> I opened its aorta to release
> The stream of consciousness.
>
> When it bled out, the rocks of Cronagorma
> Bloomed magenta and a nightingale
> From the Black Woods, perched on a cairn,
> Started to sing.
> – 'The Blue Stacks'

The self-mockery in this poem leads one to understand that the play with contradiction and juxtaposed image-patterns is just that – play. But in Ms. Steppe's poetry there's always the undertow of tragic irony; some of the playfulness leads to serious realisations. The haunting cover portrait, by Catherine Arnold, of a young woman staring into firelight, takes on powerful resonances from the first poem, 'Ascension', as well as 'Tiger Lily', 'I Will Go Now', and several more of these singularly impressive, exciting poems.

Michael S Begnal

Gràdh, Grá, Grá

Somhairle MacGill-Eain/Sorley MacLean, *Dàin do Eimhir*, edited by
Christopher Whyte, The Association for Scottish Literary Studies,
2002, pb. £12.95.
*Furnace of Love: A Selection from the Religious Poetry of Tadhg Gaelach
Ó Súilleabháin*, translated by Pádraig J. Daly, Dedalus, 2002, pb. €8.00.
Biddy Jenkinson, *Mis*, Coiscéim, 2001, pb. €5.08.

Somhairle MacGill-Eain (aka Sorley MacLean) is recognised as the
foremost modern Scottish Gaelic poet, and *Dàin do Eimhir*, his cycle of
love poems, has come to be seen as his masterpiece. Yet it constitutes
an elusive work on almost every level. Published only in part during
his lifetime, MacGill-Eain felt uneasy about many of the poems in the
Dàin, and moved to withhold a number of them from the public
domain. If MacGill-Eain's original editor Douglas Young had not
refused orders to destroy certain items, the cycle would still contain
important gaps. Luckily he did refuse, and Christopher Whyte (editor
of the present volume) has managed to track down all but one of the
missing poems from manuscript and other sources, making this the
most comprehensive version of the *Dàin* ever published.

The fact that its author took against his own work cannot be ignored.
MacGill-Eain was a committed Communist who had wished to join
the fight against Franco during the Spanish Civil War, and eventually
did fight against fascism in the Second World War. However, the love
wrangles that inspired many of these poems were often to take
precedence over the poet's political principles, and this appears to
have been a major source of tension not only in his life but also in the
cycle itself. As MacGill-Eain writes in 'Dàn IV',

> A nighean a' chùil bhuidhe, throm-bhuidh, òr-bhuidh,
> fonn do bheòil-sa 's gaoir na h-Eòrpa,
> a nighean gheal chasarlach aighearach bhòidheach,
> cha bhiodh masladh ar latha-ne searbh 'nad phòig-sa.

(Girl of the yellow, heavy-yellow, gold-yellow hair, / the song of your mouth
and Europe's shivering cry, / fair, heavy-haired, spirited, beautiful girl, / the
disgrace of our day would not be bitter in your kiss.)

This poem sets the tone for much of the work, the poet alternatively declaring his love for the two or three real-life Eimhirs, and excoriating himself for his failure to sacrifice himself for his political beliefs.

The knowledge that MacGill-Eain later considered his love poetry to be a 'bourgeois' preoccupation must certainly colour our view of the *Dàin*. But can the author justifiably expect to retain such strict control over his work? Should his wishes have been respected, and the pieces that he withdrew as too personally revealing be left unpublished? In his introduction, Whyte quotes Derick Thomson on this particular matter: 'When that work was published, it passed out of the control of its author. It became a literary fact not subject to distortion or second thoughts'. In this instance the present reviewer is inclined to agree. *Dàin do Eimhir* appears to be that sort of phenomenon, the thing that is bigger than its creator.

Nonetheless, serious concerns about the text remain, not least of which has to do with the question of translation. The majority of readers unable to read the original Gaelic are getting a second-hand MacGill-Eain, mediated through two varieties of English translation (the author's own, and in some cases the editor's literal renderings). For the Irish reader who speaks Irish, the Gaelic is approachable enough when you have the English to fall back on. Still, unless you are a fluent Gaelic speaker, reading this is a kind of patchwork – start with a few lines of the original, then over to the English when you're stuck on a word, then to the notes at the back of the book. The editor insists that it shouldn't be viewed firstly as a translation; it is 'emphatically an edition with commentary of the Gaelic text, and not of the English versions, even when the latter have been prepared by MacLean'. This is quite an admirable assertion, actually, but then why is the commentary in English? Reasons of accessibility are given, though the editor is not unaware of the contradictions inherent in this approach. We still end up having to contextualise MacGill-Eain's Gaelic poems in a language vastly different from that in which they were composed.

With its copious annotations, footnotes, appendices and textual variations, the present volume sometimes resembles Vladimir Nabokov's *Pale Fire*. Ostensibly we're meant to be reading a long poetic sequence, but there's so much going on elsewhere in the book. Whyte's notes are often quite illuminating, pointing out MacGill-Eain's sources, quoting letters and criticism, suggesting interpretations and so on. At the same time they steer our reading in a particular direction, usually Whyte's own. Certainly, though, we can trust Whyte much more than the clearly unreliable Charles Kinbote of Nabokov's novel, despite such delectably irrelevant comments as in this annotation to the phrase 'am bial mòr bàn' ('the great white mouth') in Dàn XLII: 'Although MacLean speaks of the beach as being pale or white, it is in reality composed of black boulders rounded by the sea and of fine, almost black sand'. In the end, it remains uncertain whether or not we can really get a firm grip on *Dàin do Eimhir*, given the nature of the text and its fluctuating history in both published and unpublished form.

None of this, though, is to say that you can't read the book and form your own impression. That's the fun of it. It will probably mostly be read in translation, but that's not the end of the world either; the important thing is that it is read. *Dàin do Eimhir* is a work of major importance, and an eminently human book. For MacGill-Eain here, at least for now, indeed almost despite himself, love is ultimately more important than ideology, the act of poetic creation more redeeming even than the just cause. As Whyte points out in the commentary, these poems 'are not just a narrative of frustrated love, but also a conscious record of the realisation of a literary vocation'.

Tadhg Gaelach Ó Súilleabháin (1715-1795) wrote secular love poems as well, but later in life devoted himself to religious themes. The title *Furnace of Love* comes from the 'Poem of Jesus' and is a metaphor for Jesus in Mary's womb. Nonetheless, translator Pádraig J Daly prominently cites Úna Nic Éinrí who, in a recent study, has drawn parallels between the language of Tadhg Gaelach's secular work and his later religious poetry. In 'The Saviour's Poem', for instance, the poet refers to Jesus as 'My Darling' and 'My Dearest' (among other, more pious epithets) and declares, 'You're my love beyond all love, King of Splendour. / Your gaze takes my love, your gait takes my love...' Nuns are exhorted to 'burn up with love, / Leap with holy excitement...' (presumably there were nuns under the age of 65 in eighteenth-century Ireland). Elsewhere, in 'Poem of Jesus', Mary is referred to as having 'Shining Breasts' (wow!) and in 'A Prayer to Mary' as being 'sweet-tasting'.

Any hint of sexuality, however, has been fully sublimated to a religious passion. As Daly (an Augustinian priest) tells us in his preface, this similarity in vocabulary between Tadhg Gaelach's secular and religious poems will come as 'no surprise to people even vaguely familiar with "The Song of Songs" or with the Christian mystics'. The poet goes to great lengths to censure himself for his earlier sinful life as a 'misguided marauder', hyperbolically claiming in 'Amen, O Jesus': 'I it was who hammered the nails / Through your fragrant feet...' But it's this sort of intensity which makes for exciting poetry. Christ's wounds gush blood, Mary 'suckle[s] so generously and nurturingly' ('Your good breasts pour out on your good family'), while St Declan is described in terms of a Gaelic chieftain in battle. Though many of us would prefer not to have to sublimate anything to begin with, Tadhg Gaelach projects a religiosity of a much wilder nature than the antiseptic version on offer from the official Church today.

The only real drawback to *Furnace of Love*, which is the first in Dedalus's Waxwing Series, is the absence of Tadhg's original Irish poems. It would be nice to compare these to the translations on facing pages. For example, when you come upon the phrase 'choking in lavatory odours' in 'The Poem of Mary', it's only natural to wonder what Tadhg Gaelach himself actually wrote. Is this a euphemism chosen by Daly in place of something more scatological? Unless we're going to search the library for the original, we don't know. We do know that Daly succeeds in living up to the standards he sets himself in his preface – that Tadhg's note of 'unfeigned love for God, his heartbroken empathy with the suffering Jesus and his passionate devotion to God's mother' has been carried over emphatically into English.

Biddy Jenkinson's is the only work presently under consideration that avoids the translation issue completely, though the contemporary Irish-language poet's wide-ranging vocabulary occasionally sent me to the dictionary. *Mis* is the poetical retelling of a post-mediaeval romance. Mis, the eponymous protagonist, is the daughter of Dáire Déadgheal, whose body she finds lying dead after the battle of Fionntrá (Ventry). This drives her insane and she becomes a horrible, clawed, bird-like monster despoiling the country around Sliabh Mis in Kerry. The king of Munster offers a reward to anyone who can tame her, and finally the harper Dubhrois arrives. There then follows a long sequence wherein

Mis is slowly mesmerised by the power of the music:

> D'fhaireas na méara leabhaire
> ag suirí leis na sreanga
> is thuigeas go mba mhéanar
> do théada na cláirsí. Thógas
> trí choiscéim ina comhair.

(I watched the pliant fingers / wooing the strings / and understood that / those harp chords were happy. I took / three steps closer.)

Dubhrois appears as a sort of Orpheus figure with the power to control the forces of nature through his art. Yet it is via sexual intercourse that Mis finally becomes human again. There's a rather funny description at this point of Dubhrois's male member, which oddly enough is being circled by a swarm of bees. 'An amhlaidh go bhfuil mil ann?' ('Could there be honey in it?'), remarks Mis. In contrast to Tadhg Gaelach Ó Súilleabháin's late-period worldview, overt sexuality in earlier Gaelic literature (and for Biddy Jenkinson here) is redemptive and renewing. Mis falls in love with Dubhrois, they get married, and Mis comes to be considered the most beautiful woman in Munster. When Dubhrois is later killed, however, Mis returns to her previous monstrous existence: 'lem chleití flichreocha / síos liom in aon bhrat oighir, / an dá chois crochta asam / mar phrátaí seaca...' ('with my frozen feathers / down me like a cloak of ice, / my feet bent out from me / like frosty potatoes...')

Mis contains much of the raw material of life, yet it is a slim volume – 35 pages – and could have stood to be a bit longer if it was to carry the weight of epic. Important events in the story are glossed over, like Dubhrois's death. Mis's time amongst the Munster elite is dispatched in a couple of sentences. There were many interesting possibilities here that were not grasped. Apparently Jenkinson sought to limit her scope. Key moments, though, are handled well, and this builds up a psychological portrait of the protagonist. Mis is a female Sweeny in a way, living in the trees, driven mad by the spectre of violence and death (though she's certainly no feminist icon – all she really needed was the love of a good man!). Jenkinson deserves plaudits for reviving this obscure figure from Irish legend; her little book resonates.

David Butler

Four Debuts and a Reappearance

Allison Eir Jenks, *The Palace of Bones*, Ohio University Press, 2002, pb. $12.95.
Liz McSkeane, *Snow at the Opera House*, New Island, 2002, pb. €8.99.
Aidan Rooney-Céspedes, *Day Release*, Gallery Books, 2000, pb. €10.09.
Anne Dean, *Odysseus in the Bathroom*, Bradshaw Books, 2002, pb. €10.
Anthony Wilson, *Nowhere Better Than This*, Worple Press, pb. £9 / €14.

In terms of their Contents pages, debut collects of poetry have begun to acquire a remarkable predictability over the past two decades. It seems it is nowadays *de rigueur*, in addition to observations from nature, to childhood memorabilia, and to second-person poems which both address and re-assess family members, to include also a substantial selection of poems which draw inspiration from experiences of cultural-tourism. At their best, these can be insightful investigations into a different dimension of identity. At their worst, they read like a hagiography of artists and exotic place-names. It goes without saying that, within this sub-genre, it is originality and use of language that confer authority and not the particular demiurges that have been invoked.

In her impressive debut collection *The Palace of Bones*, the young American poet Allison Eir Jenks makes notable use of an extended stay in Ireland (many of the poems in her collection were begun at the Tyrone Guthrie Centre in Annaghmakerrig) and a visit to the Louvre to mount just such a questioning of her own identity. Her poem 'Waiting' is a meditation on womanhood triggered by Kathy Prendergast's sculpture of the same name presently on show in the Hugh Lane Gallery. The language of the opening is assertive: 'Who with a human soul wouldn't notice / Three women against a wall with melted heads, / Dressed obediently...', yet the poem also finds room to consider the women's complicity in their situation: 'you do not wait / As martyrs or as ghosts, you are willing / To be chosen...'

In similar vein, the title poem refers to that hurried visit made to 'the Louvre, / The ghosts of history confined / In one heavy album full of eyes.' In a startling conceit that refers to the *Mona Lisa* ('monarch, token / of womanhood'), Jenks notes how 'Strangers crowded around her/

Like the hanging of a witch'. Juxtaposed, in memory at least, is the portrait of a female martyr. But Jenks is not so much concerned here with presenting a feminist critique of western art *per se*. To an extent, she too is the voyeuse, 'browsing blissfully / Into her glass for my own reflection.'

If it is true that, for the poet, 'Even now these women trouble me, / Dancing like a string of pearls / That will never clasp…', they are part of an entire nexus of experiences and relationships which are presented with both an enviable command of language and a deep emotional ambivalence. With reference to her sister, in a poem entitled 'The Little Red Schoolhouse', there is a helpless anger in the imagery, and in the final enjambment of 'Every nail I punch into the wall / To hang a pretty new painting, / / I wish I were nailing her back / To when she didn't know Dad / Would leave and Mom go crazy'; while in a later poem, 'Stained Dresses', that deals with the mother's old age, the absence of communication is highlighted by the rhetorical third-person: 'Does she pretend to have vanished / As I lift her heavy body from the bath?'

Liz McSkeane tries out a number of masks in the course of her first collection, *Snow at the Opera House*. In Section I: a childless aunt on the Titanic; the 'woman in the attic' from Jane Eyre; in Section II: a victim of an execution squad; an Omagh shopper. The flexibility of style and perspective is noteworthy, though more successful and of greater interest (as are the poems generally) in the opening section. McSkeane has a fine sense of menace, and it is put to most effective use when the subject is domestic. The strongest poem in the collection, impressive by any standards, is the disconcerting meditation on beauty, 'Butterflies' ('Everyone else seems to love them. / They give me the creeps – all that fluttering…'), while an anecdote about a trapped magpie that follows this poem ('Don't let / me know if he made it or not, not yet.') is far more engaging than, say, 'A Young Man Has Been Sentenced to Death' in Section II.

Elsewhere, McSkeane is particularly effective in her use of the mimetic potential of poetry. The repetitions and circularities of the poem 'Snap!' economically suggest those of the medium of photography, while the sense of claustrophobia and vulnerability imagined on entering

Harlech Castle are succinctly captured (excuse the pun) by successive enjambment: 'By now a portcullis would have barred / the way back and another crashed down ahead / of where I'm standing at the barest hint / that anyone unwelcome or who didn't / have a reason to be there, was there…' When she plays to her strengths, McSkeane has the gift of enabling us to see afresh.

Another poet who exploits the mimetic potential of the medium is Aidan Rooney-Céspedes. The three increasingly lengthy sentences that go to make up the '12th July' mirror the children's tentative revival of the sectarian bonfire on the morning after, while the poem 'Bumping Cars' becomes almost a study in onomatopoeia: '…The chrome mast rasps its stylus / on the electric grille, scratching sparks across / the ceiling.' Rooney-Céspedes has also a fine sense of how to allow imagery carry multiple-meaning. The poem 'Harry', the portrait of a mental hospital patient to whom the collection's title in part alludes, finishes: 'He showered my wellingtons / with a jet of piss, his day's hot release / before he drove back, his wheels' mucked chevrons / zipping shut the backroads to the Mental.'

When the poems of Rooney-Céspedes move between locations, as for instance Monaghan and France, there is a concomitant semantic shift which is itself the centre of interest (he teaches French at the Thayer Academy, Massachusetts). This is perhaps more obvious when one is familiar with the poetry that he has written since *Day Release* came out in September 2000. Within the collection, though, poems such as '*Vitrier*', 'Encounter at Les Bories' and the impressive 'Magic Antennae' ('Right here they shot the scene in which a *flic*, // in hot pursuit, houses a *balle fatale* / in the head of a gangster whose *meurtres* / have shook the backstreets of *Montmartre*...') cleverly explore the dimension of the familiar and the distinct in another linguistic culture. Even within the English language, Rooney-Céspedes' work has a formal restlessness and versatility that reminds one perhaps of Ciaran Carson or Paul Muldoon.

There is a thin line in art between the economical and the parsimonious, and many of Anne Dean's pieces hath a lean and hungry look. This is not a matter of word count as such. It is rather that, where a poem uses minimal imagery, the language itself must do a great deal of work if the piece is not to appear trivial. When too great a number of poems finish on phrases of three or fewer words, as is the case in *Odysseus in the Bathroom*, the cumulative effect on the reader can be that the poet is being excessively pat.

The collection is also the one which relies most heavily on allusions to artists and to foreign place-names. Throughout the latter half, the 'Baedeker effect' becomes particularly intrusive. This is unfortunate. In poems such as 'Her Point of View' and 'Madame Cézanne' ('I picked the first apples / in a far off orchard. He saw me, / sketched me, eyes luminous, / charcoal shades in my hair'), Dean displays an original perspective and a fine command of language.

Finally, to a book which is not a debut collection, and which, curiously, was up to a point the most disappointing of the five. In his third collection, *Nowhere Better Than This*, Anthony Wilson occasionally displays a very real poetic gift. The understated detail of 'Beatings were frequent and public. / One boy drowned himself in the swimming pool in December. / The water was black and full of leaves', from a poem entitled 'His Training for the Mission Field Remembered', is evidence of considerable talent. A similar restraint is at work in the following, from 'Wedding Day': 'A pair of black shoes in the hall, and my father speaking softly about loss.'

More often, however, the impression that this collection gives is one of glibness. The excessive employment of loose speech patterns, slangy allusions, and titles such as 'The Small Provincial City Open Mic Poetry Thing' are apt after a while to leave one cold. The use of a colloquial voice is not in itself a bad thing; it becomes a problem when one comes away from a book with the feeling that craft has been too often set to one side.

Brian Coffey

Of Denis Devlin: Vestiges, Sentences, Presages
[This article was first published in the *University Review*, Vol, II, No.11, in 1960, edited by Lorna Reynolds. It is reprinted here with the kind permission of the poet's son, John Coffey. In the original article, quotations were referenced to the collection in which the quote appeared, with no mention of the poem's title. In this reprint, the quotes are referenced to the title of the poem, and to the page in the *Collected Poems* (The Dolmen Press, 1964) where the quote appears].

1. *Bibliography.*
Poems, Brian Coffey and Denis Devlin: privately printed, Dublin, 1930.
Intercessions, Denis Devlin: Europa Press, London, 1937.
Translations from Saint-John Perse, Denis Devlin: *Rains*, 'The Sewanee Review', 1945; *Snows*, New York, 1945; *Exile and Other Poems*, Pantheon Books, New York, 1949. *Lough Derg and Other Poems*, Denis Devlin: New York, Reynal and Hitchcock, 1946.
'The Heavenly Foreigner', Denis Devlin: *Poetry Ireland*, Dublin, 1950.
Translations from Réne Char, Denis Devlin and Jackson Mathews: *Botteghe Oscure*, X, Rome, 1952.
'The Colours of Love', Denis Devlin: *Botteghe Oscure*, X, Rome, 1952.
'The Passion of Christ', Denis Devlin, *Encounter*, London, 1957 [as per *Collected Poems*].
'Memoirs of a Turcoman Diplomat', Denis Devlin: *Botteghe Oscure*, XXIV, Rome, 1959.
'Mr. Allen', Denis Devlin: *The Irish Times*, Dublin, 1958 [as per *Collected Poems*].

In addition to the works listed above, there exist manuscripts of some unfinished poems in English, the manuscript of poems translated from the French into Gaelic verse (by Denis Devlin and Niall Montgomery in collaboration), and, possibly, poems published in reviews and not yet collected, or unpublished poems in the possession of friends. The forthcoming American edition of Denis's work will not, I believe, take the place of a much-to-be-desired critical edition of the *Collected Poems*, the publication of which might well be done in Ireland [Editorial Note: *Collected Poems*, ed. by Brian Coffey, was published by The Dolmen Press,1964].

2. Once, when we were students in Paris, Denis said that I should have to write about him one day. It was easy said in one of those moments when young men share out golden mountains, masteries, domains, futures, fortunes even. But Denis did not foresee the real future. Replace the lecture-halls of the Sorbonne and the laughing group of friends in the unscrupulously appropriate *Bar du Départ* by spheres of responsibility and power among men of like attainment and quality –

you have done no more than substitute one commonplace expression by another. In the real future, as we know now, we discover one who is loved about to address his only lover, the peace of lovers upon which it is not wise to intrude.

There would have been obviously good reasons for a reluctance on my part to write a set piece about the friend whom I had not seen for twelve years before his shockingly sudden death. It is a fact, however, that apart from members of Denis's family, there was no one who was more closely associated with Denis during the years of his deliberate choices in poetry than myself. I may, then, attempt to relate the Denis of that period to the man whose latest poems earn for him, as I judge, a unique place among poets writing in English during the present century. And in the first place, therefore, dates and anecdotes not unnecessary.

3. Autumn, 1928: Founding of the UCD Dramatic Society. About this time my brother Donough introduced me to Denis whom he had brought home after a rehearsal. Denis and I became close companions with a common interest in poetry, a common outlet for our verses in the National Student and the opportunity which, in the grand style, our college offered for unending discussion with our contemporaries – while the lecturers were lecturing for all they were worth inside – outside on the main-entrance steps. Mervyn Wall, a friend since those good days, has caught exactly the atmosphere of the situation in his contribution to the history of the L & H.

4. September, 1930: Publication of *Poems* by Brian Coffey and Denis Devlin. We published at our own expense, at a cost of approximately £12-10-0, in an edition of 250 copies (with a pre-publication reprint of 100 copies – so that no one would miss getting his copy in the rush, that wonderful rush). Mr. Nairn of Combridge's treated us very kindly, helping us to reach the public. Ultimately, although we had more than one hundred copies left unsold, we did clear costs.

The poems included in the volume were not, as is so frequently said, the result of a collaboration. In the summer of 1930 Denis had four poems completed and I had five. We both felt that something should be done to show that the pre-treaty tradition of writing from UCD was not dead. The volume was a device for putting our work quickly into print (we were both on the point of leaving college), since we should otherwise have had to wait indefinitely upon the notice of review editors for publication. The volume did get a few gentle reviews. Denis sent a copy to Robert Graves, whose poetry we both greatly admired. The letter (now lost, I regret to say) which came back (jet-black ink on rough paper) from Deyá reiterated the I-distrust-and-dislike-the-Irishness of Mr. Graves, while there was praise for the 'natural intelligence' of Mr. Devlin who, the writer of the letter hoped, 'would unrelate (himself) further.'

Having achieved *Poems*, following a good send-off from Fear-na-Cnoc in his *Sunday Independent* college column, we both felt justified in calling ourselves poets. He knew we did not yet qualify under Ben Jonson's definition: 'Those are poets, the poor fellows who live by it.' I find it very moving that, in a letter of May 9th, 1959, Denis wrote to me: 'I am making a great effort to get a book together – at least, then, one needn't look sheepish or enraged when nice people nicely ask one – "Well, where can I find your poems?" '

5. Autumn, 1930: Denis went on Travelling Studentship to Munich. We met for a few days in Strasbourg, Easter, 1931. Denis was full of his new experiences:

> It was a heady springtime in Munich
> Many I knew confided in me
> Popu, the champion cyclist
> Sigmund, deriding tyrants
> And Carlos...
>   – 'Little Elegy', p. 82

Denis enjoyed what he called the put-together-ness of Munich, its guide-book-like assortment of architectures, the element of all mankind realised in the students from many lands there assembled (and how grown up these people seemed after innocent student Dublin). Also he encountered anti-semitism in practice and he never forgot the experience.

The following June or July, he passed through Paris on his way home, separating then from the young woman...

> I love your eyelids, leaves landing...
>   – 'Edinburgh Tale, p. 78

...whose features, whose presence – precincts of attractive power – quickened in Denis the image of the object of love:

> Why must, as absence ages, she all the more instant cling?
>> – 'Farewell and Good', p. 85

6: Autumn, 1931: Denis went to Paris where I already was. He stayed there, with short breaks, for two years. It was noticeable from the start how rapidly a group of companions would form itself around Denis. In such a company, of an evening, gaiety (it happened often and often) would move someone to sing the first song. If it was Denis who began, always, with matching gestures, he would sing a rowing song of Aran: "Ó ró mo bháidín ag snámh ar an gcuan." I have heard songs in as many as eight different languages during one such evening.

In Spring, 1932, Denis and a friend, Sam Pope Brewer, the American journalist, visited Spain together. They returned after three weeks, looking very thin, because money had run out some days before. But the visit (I do not know if it was ever repeated) made a deep impression on Denis, making more exact, broader, more detailed the imagery (based on his reading), which he had condensed around his Munich friend, Carlos. Denis's Spain has been captured in his 'Meditation at Avila', *Collected Poems*, p. 53).

When, early in 1933, if I remember correctly (for I cannot lay hands on a copy of the book, to check), *Poems* by Niall Sheridan and Donagh McDonagh reached us, we were delighted as much by the excellence of those first verses as by the thought that it had been good example to publish from UCD.

Three persons whom Denis met during his Paris years require to be mentioned. There was Gaston Bonheur, who at the age of eighteen seemed to us to have mastered the problem of a personal verse style in poems in which he used an imagery wholly derived from his birthplace in the Montagne Noire, near Carcassonne (*Chemin Privé* by Gaston Bonheur, Paris, 1933). Denis admired greatly one poem which began:

> Canton d'Axat au fond du monde
> battu par la houle does rocailles
> Les femmes vont à la forêt du Fange
> où les hommes ne vont jamais deux fois
>> – loc. cit., p. 20

Gaston was M. Pierre Guéguen's helper in founding and running a small review, *14 RUE DU DRAGON*, in which French translations of early poems by Denis appear.

Then there was Roger Bullion. Roger had spent five years, he told us, in the Foreign Legion, having run away from home. He turned out to have an exact taste in French verse and some poetic ability. He said (on an occasion when Denis had been reciting the 'Mignonne, allons voir si la rose' of Ronsard: "que je vous envie de pouvoir vous approcher de ces choses comme pour la première fois." Under Denis's encouragement, Bullion began to write again. In the course of about six months he produced a collection of poems in which the influence of Eluard does not swamp the lyrical impulse for which Bullion was well endowed – he lacked only abiding purpose to bring his gifts to their best use. Denis kept copies of the poems. They were full of what the French call *trouvailles*. I remember one group of verses:

> toi trouble montée de mes yeux
> toi l'animée du buisson bourdonnant
> toi forme en forme de fouet
> toi somneil des pavés clairs.

The relationship with Bullion was characteristic of Denis who encouraged many poets to use their talents more perfectly. A talent should be vindicated, he said. An occasional companion of this kind would turn out to lack the seriousness of a poet, being merely amusing, like the one who shouted, while he sat: "How can I talk, without a drink in my hand?"

Lastly, there was Tom McGreevy. Meeting Tom was an important event in both our lives. We had, each of us, as we would learn, gained an unfailing, understanding friend. But at the time of first meetings, we appreciated in Tom the poet of excellent craftmanship and delicate kind feeling; we admired the critic of wide, accurate and unexpected knowledge who listened so patiently to the views of our inexperience; and we began then to undergo a formation in literature and art which none but Tom could have effected. For who but Tom has assimilated into the Catholic outlook of a Southern Irishman the intellectual and artistic traditions of wider distant Europe for which Irish Catholics, bypassing the other island, have always felt an affinity. Tom, the older man, unlike the WB Yeats whom one believes to have rejoiced in conflict for its own sake, we found – it is admirable – to have fought and suffered personally for good principles. To meet Tom meant, for both of us, passage from the 'great, blooming, buzzing confusion' of inexperience into regions of control.

7. Summer, 1933: Denis returned to Dublin. The time of our continuous association had come to an end. Denis was appointed lecturer, in the Department of English at UCD, and there he lectured in the following year to 'full houses' He would have made his mark in academic life, there can be no doubt of it. For family reasons, he decided to leave university life and take up the diplomatic career, entering the Department of Foreign Affairs in 1936. Prior to this, he spent some time on the Greater Blasket, in order to improve his knowledge of Gaelic. From this period also dates the translation of French poems into Gaelic verse in which he and Niall Montgomery collaborated.

I returned from Paris in the summer of 1936, hoping (with a hope which for far too many Irishmen to-day still seems to lie beyond the scope of practical politics) to make a living and a home in Ireland. Actually, and the manner of it still offends me, that hope was not realised. I saw Denis occasionally, nearly always in some quiet place where we would discuss problems of poetry. But Denis was a busy man, whose social life was developing, while I was preoccupied with personal problems and anxious to avoid social commitments:

> Busy, alone, we all go far and wide
> Who once listened to each other's
> Fair vows and counsel.
>   – 'Little Elegy', p. 83

Thus, when Denis, on the occasion of Mr. Austin Clarke's return to Dublin, asked me to go with him to a meeting of Irish poets for the purpose of welcoming the older, established poet home, I declined, so that Mr. Clarke, whose poetry, thanks to Mr. JJ O'Neill, Librarian at UCD, I had known for years, might well have suspected hostility, where none was intended, in my not attending the meeting.

In October, 1937, I left Dublin. Subsequently, I met Denis four or five times and last of all in 1947, after his marriage, when he introduced me to his pretty, charming and vivacious wife, Caren. I met Caren next about a month after Denis's death to discuss matters connected with the literary executorship. Almost all of Denis's greatest poetry dates from the years of his marriage with Caren.

To conclude this section: Denis was not a good correspondent, nor was I. A dozen letters and postcards are all that we exchanged in nearly thirty years. What we did not exchange were the letters we wrote and did not dispatch. There were many such, on each side.

* * *

8. The following sections refer to aspects of Denis's character and behaviour which seem to me to have some bearing on the poet and his poetry. (I'm not presuming to exhaust the subject).

9. Denis did not go out of his way to engineer meetings with writers in whom he was interested. He felt sure that he would meet those whom he would need to meet – in due course.

10. He was naturally endowed for sympathising with others – mysterious endowment of biological and of intellectual quality; attention to what others were and to what they needed became a virtue in Denis, a life-time's practice of which was rewarded in his poetry by the marvel of:

> One, Simon, in excess of passion,
> Trusted his unreflecting hands;
> What is this genius of compassion
> That comprehends, nor understands!
> > – 'The Passion of Christ', p. 12

11. His love of justice: hinted at in his dislike of gossip, more firmly featured in his care not to give scandal, fed at the level of literary expression, on the bardic and political poetry of Ireland, on the Psalms, on his reading of history: must have developed strongly in the home surroundings, both in Scotland and in Ireland during the pre-treaty days. His 'Argument with Justice' comes to the formal apostrophic conclusion of poetic, not political judgement:

> Virtue of all men, fear not that we thy temple crumble,
> > flesh crumbles, but
> Not till the mind's raped out. Fear rather thy name be

> forgotten from father to
> Son, or by the saints. Come down, let there be
> Justice though the heavens fall, be virtue of our
> Temporary measure.
> > – 'Argument with Justice', p. 59

12. Ritual: At one time he lodged in the Hotel de l'Avenir, rue Gay Lussac. I found him there, one afternoon *the* blue notebook on the table before him, pen in hand, duster on his head, pyjamas on over his clothes, mouth compressed (as always when his hand held a pen ready to write – or even in the act of reading). Silence, resumed after greetings, was suddenly broken by the cry: "God, let me write a poem."

13. His *docility* in face of new experience is, I think, illustrated by the following anecdote: we were having dinner at a Chinese restaurant – students can get a cheap, filling meal in Chinese restaurants – when Denis decided to try what was listed as 'Chinese pepper.' An object resembling an evaporating basin which held a sort of shallow red sludge was brought to him. Denis swallowed a spoonful and immediately began to show signs of distress, jumping, gasping, running around the room, finally drinking off the contents of a carafe of water. After some minutes, when his face had recovered its normal colour and he could be at ease again, he remarked: "Those old Chinese philosophers were subtle."

14. He had the kind of family sense and comportment, involved in conscious legalities, that one notices so frequently in France:

> I am the eldest son and my right was questioned
> > – 'The Heavenly Foreigner', p.24

He respected an 'inviolable family stone' ('Victory of Samothrace', p. 75).

He saw:

> Mother and sisters like light through glass,
> With stopped lightning stood in the arch.
> > – 'Jansenist Journey', p. 44

15. Good manners, almost courtly manners: they were the rules within which he moved physically. I have known a leave-taking when the departing companion was in such a hurry to join the new lot awaiting him below decks he could not quickly enough be rid of the companion he was with. Neither greeting nor leavetaking was unceremonious with Denis. He included standards of good-behaviour among the principles according to which he would judge poets, as men; he refers, for instance to 'the toady, Horace' ('Encounter', p. 38).

16. He could not abide the personal habit become mere body reaction or mere mental inertia, nor habit realised in vested interest or in what one may term liturgical materialism:

> Hell is to know our natural empire used
> Wrong, by mind's moulting, brute divinities.
> > – 'Lough Derg', p. 37

> How shall we suffer the little children to come unto us, how
> > shall we pay
> For the ranged, amorphous faces grey as the creased skies this
> > guttering day?
> While pushbelly, hunger-currency laymen, cultivating the
> > licorice flowers
> Of their happy entrails, dance around earth-
> > produce pyres
> And religious scarecrows navigate with downcast eyes this
> > vale of tears.
> > – 'Bacchanal', p. 62

* * *

17. There follow some notes, necessarily incomplete, on influences on Denis's literary development.

18. There was a good library (of the English classics, mainly) in the Devlin home.

19. Denis used a copy of *Longer Poems of the English Language* until it fell apart.

20. He used to enjoy Shakespeare as presented and above all as read by his English professor, Dr. O'Donovan.

21. His understanding of the French language and literature was

initially founded on what he had acquired through the inimitable lecturing technique of Roger Chauviré. Chauviré was a good poet. His lyric beginning:

J'avais un toit gris
Gris du gris de ses colombes

is a masterpiece. With a voice of great range and immediate response to intention, with gestures as good as a whole new language, Chauviré could introduce his students to the authors and to the characters of classical French literature as if to his personal friends. He was a tease. In one gorgeous piece of fireworks he declared: 'Je connais toutes les filles de joie du dixseptiéme siècle.' It was he too who owned the calm and informative voice of the figure I observed coming backward out of the tumulus at New Grange proffering to a foreign professor the fact: "Vous savez, Tutankhamun est mort de la tubérculose."

Well, from Chauviré Denis gained not only a whole culture, but in addition Racine and La Fontaine. Chauviré knew the secret of 'Les Deux Pigeons'. Chauviré knew the Alexandrine with the understanding of a good craftsman. Young French poets were always astonished by Denis's broad and detailed grasp of their literature, which he owed primarily to Roger Chauviré. Rabelais I cannot remember him being interested in. Villon he loved. He practiced Montaigne. Gide he studied carefully. Eluard he kept beside him.

22. Denis's choice was to write in English. "The English language is a great language for poetry," he said. He could read Gaelic. In one search through bardic poetry he found, he told me, just one image which bore some resemblance to a surrealist image. He was affected deeply both by the lovely 'Gile na gile' as well as by the perfect death-bed poem of Egan O'Rahilly.

He made many experiments in verse. 'Bacchanal' (*Collected Poems*, p. 60) incorporates many of the prosodic ideas which he was considering in 1933. I believe it taught him that there would be no advantage in attempting to use the full apparatus of a prosody based on both stress and a full similarity of vowel sounds in corresponding stressed syllables – especially if homogeneity of stanza or of complete poem were intended. Hyde's history of Gaelic literature, full of English imitations of Gaelic rhythmic, rhyming and alliterative schemes would – in spite of Hyde's versatility – cure any poet-reader of Saintsbury's history of English prosody (Denis was such a one) from any attempt to work right against the tradition and the spirit of English verse.

23. Denis paid close attention to the proper use and definition of English words and phrases. I have heard of him seeking information of an architect in order to clarify his understanding of the term: *oblique lighting*. His respect for all that affected the proper use of English was the respect of a man who would seek all else abroad, in France or in Spain, or in Germany or elsewhere. (Lest any false impression should be given, I place here a remark from a letter dated 25th March, 1947, written to me after his appointment to London. It should be remembered that he had spent the war years in Washington): 'After having defended the English for five years, I suddenly don't know what to make of them.' He carried no political prejudices into the private judgment hall where he decided on the modes of his uses of English for writing. In fact, I believe he was quite unwilling to accept the idea of an Irish poet related parasitically or in some symbiosis of province and capital city to the London scene. Certainly not.

24. There was a period, in Paris, when he put in a lot of work on an animal poem. He read me quite lengthy passages from this poem, which would have extended at least to two hundred verses. The writing was humourous. Where is the poem?

25. Methods in composition. When he was in Paris, Denis wrote all his poems in one blue-covered note-book. He worked slowly, word by word, verse by verse, adding, taking away, substituting, trying out again and again, endless patience, ceaseless application – one might be allowed some laxity in what was a clear matter of duty; one could not take sufficient care about those things which, although necessity was lacking, one had elected to do. His last manuscript resembles all the others, even early ones, that I have seen. They provide us with 'The evidence that lifting needles makes the cloth.' ('Death and Her Beasts, Ignoble Beasts', p. 94).

26. He worked at the level of things deindividualised without having become abstractions. For example, the 'Forerunners' in 'Bacchanal' (*Collected Poems*, p. 60) are figures realised in all times and all places, in contrast with the Audenesque 'communist orator' who 'lands at the pier' – mere topicality, here today and gone tomorrow.

27. He was a *maker of verses* from the start. When he encountered surrealism he was already protected against seduction by his past experience of versemaking. He felt the attraction of Eluard strongly. But he did not find it possible to accept surrealism and its pronouncements as explicative of Eluard's verse. He felt sure, and subsequent revelations have proved him right, that Eluard's style was the result of deliberate choices; it could never have been the uncorrected resultant of spontaneous regurgitations (or would it be gurgitations?) from the vasty depths within the person. I should judge also that it was the same verse-making experience which left him in a freer position as regards the attraction, the seductive power of *The Waste Land* than was usual at the time. He judged theories of poetry by the standards of what was required for verse-making. Possibly, the only useful theory of poetry for a poet is the one which does not supply him with any tool to misuse language with.

28. Scaffoldings have a beauty of their own which distracts the eye from the beauty of the buildings they envelop. However, in order to indicate the right soil of associative capacity from which Denis's poetry springs, I offer the following indications of the sources of terms and verses: (a) (from 'Windtacker Windjamming', p. 95):

> My thoughts get such a shock
> They set up a most undignified screaming
> Like a lot of schoolboy factory horns at one o'clock.

The factory horns were heard by Denis in a composition for reduced orchestra written by Stravinsky and entitled, I believe, *Barcelona One O'Clock*.

(b) (from 'Gradual', p. 97):

> Lighthouse, O regent of the seas trampling

The word 'regent' was present to Denis in the verse from Villon:

> Dame des cieulx, regente terrienne.

He wanted to use the term with something of the movement its French equivalent acquires in Villon's verse. Why, it may be asked. Answer, because a poet falls in love with single words.

(c) The rhythms and stresses of Denis's verse often echo rhythms he found in French poets. Thus:

> This woman who passes by, sideways, by your side:
> There was one you loved for years and years...
>> – 'Memoirs of a Turcoman Diplomat', p.3

echoes the following verses from Apollinaire's 'Zone' which Denis had often attempted to translate:

> ...une jeune fille que tu trouves belie et qui est laide
> Elle doit se marier avec un étudiant de Leyde.

29. Punctuation. Denis followed the example set by Mallarmé, in the 'Eventails', without going quite as far as Mallarmé, who, in the poems referred to, does not punctuate at all – quite a sensible procedure if like Mallarmé, one has a theory about the use of the blank spaces on a page. In his latest work, Denis punctuates heavily, hoping thus to achieve, I presume, a greater control over others in their speaking of his verse.

30. Shortly before his death, he wrote: 'It's really pointless writing except to be read.'

31. He sought a perfectly controlled utterance, in order to announce what existed in his world, which is our world seen his way, his way of seeing being our best of seeing, when he is at his best:

> The Sava and the Danube were like two horses folded, mane on mane,
> And there were dogs which lapped the water up:
> Pale sunlight and pale water, as if some great poet
> Said there was peace, like Goethe, and there was peace.
>> – 'Memoirs of a Turcoman Diplomat', p. 7

32. He satisfied himself about the worth of metrical eccentricities early on, while writing 'Now' (*Collected Poems*, p. 116). This poem, which appeared first in the National Student, was the object of heated arguments. The 'blue-flamed serpent' which coiled itself around the filled 'Urn of the Occident' in the first two verses, induced apoplectic explosions in two souls. Thank goodness for the National Student which allowed a poet to sow his metrical wild oats.

33. Every poet of originality finishes by defining a new universe of images. Denis's imagery is extremely rich, drawing in a complex manner, which only example can demonstrate, on the whole range of human sensing:

> The tendrils of fountain water thread that silk music
> > – 'The Statue and the Perturbed Burghers', p. 40

> Already immense shoulders heave edgeways through heavy
> > bales of sleep
> > > – 'Bacchanal', p. 62

Referring to 'curious Death':

> Now your corrupt sweet pleading through my friends
> Smoothes me like cambric on an infant's flesh
> > – 'Death and Her Beasts, Ignoble Beasts', p.93

Influenced by Dali:

> Metamorphosis, pheasants into beating
> Horses love-abreast...
> > – 'Gradual', p. 97

A complete figure develops:

> Let's have breakfast now to pretend it's morning
> No, the bell corrodes the silence cover my mouth
> Gentle when I am sleeping breathe O summer twilight
> The fireflies of your gentle thoughts through my gnarled
> > thorntree nerves
> Smile through my eyelids soothing as a shaded lamp.
> > – 'Communication from the Eiffel Tower', p. 99-100

In the later poems image is nearly always in subordination to the total figure, though felicities occur again and again, for example:

> The pigeons growl like dogs in sleep remote.
> – 'Colours of Love', p. 18

Denis realised finally a verse texture so perfect that there is no longer any question of breaking the verse down into its constituent tricks; for example:

> When Spring with her lambs and sea-cries rises,
> Her fluent fantasy makes a mock of me;
> I throw off my absolutist devices
> And dissemble in the loose resplendent sea...
> – 'Colours of Love', p. 20

34. Denis managed a great variety of styles easily. His metrical virtuosity, his wit, the gravity, eloquence, tenderness of his language, his sarcasm, have all been noticed by reviewers. Niall Sheridan has pointed out how effectively Denis could load the 'banal, colloquial phrase with such overtones of pathos and irony.' Denis worked through a variety of themes; love and death, time and change, the woman, such themes as are common to all lyrical poets, and differently used by each. His themes of *justice* and *family* are more rarely used by poets. In keeping with his understanding of the bardic task, Denis satirised, frequently as, for example:

> Their mutual shirtfronts gleamed in a white smile
> Their electorate at breakfast approved of the war for peace
> And the private detective idly deflowered a rose.
> – 'Anteroom: Geneva', p. 58

He can join satire to pity:

> When leaves have fallen and there's nothing left
> But plainsong from ascetic bony birds,
> I say a prayer for all who are bereft
> Of love, of leafy summer, of loving words.
> – 'Colours of Love', p. 20

He will judge:

Divinities of my youth,
Expound to me my truth;

Whether from Judah or Rome
Or my nearer Gaeldom.

[...]

But divinities of my youth,
You can no longer tell the truth,

It is too much a struggle to
Keep quality confined to you.

– 'Colours of Love', p. 20

There is, in fact, behind his use of other already named themes, another theme, that of loves in conflict, which is fundamental to the poetry of Denis.

* * *

35. The maker of a poem is always *all* of the man who made it. 'Agens...totius et partis est ille qui dictus est, et totaliter videtur esse.' (Dante, *Tutte le Opere*, Oxford, 1904: Epist. X, 261-2).

36. How is the agent placed in the initial instant of his activity? Denis wrote (1933) during a period when he took part in experiments and exercises designed to check the pronouncements of surrealism: 'The meditation which I make and which then seems to me to be necessary to be formed poetically is always an excited joy of life in action. It is never reasonable; the sentences in which it is clothed are never complete but run unfinished and impatient one into the other imperiously casting off the necessity of logical finish. When I actually work, almost always the first word is of a sorrowful mood.' Thus he states the mysterious in the beginnings of poetry, what textual studies and the rediscovery of scaffoldings are incompetent to make clearer than life itself.

36. *The poet* goes to his task prepared – a man endowed, individual, a person, one agent – not to be categorized as separated into a body and a soul, not seeing himself as thus categorized. He has an immense capacity for liquefaction, for changing into all things, like the sea suffused with stars, pearly with light, and for changing all things, like a drop of blood spreading to colour the whole sea. The marvellous sensibility of a Denis restores under personal seal all the multitude of realities it has accepted, matched and mated with, suffered through, in its willing advance towards, immersion in, reception of all existing things. Always it issues forth finally in poems, always the first utterance is inchoate. Precise utterance is the reward of labour.

37. At the source of the poem Denis found a mystery of loving-knowing, no dependancy of logic or of wintry moral sense, no matter-of-fact beloved of cockahoop positive sparrows. The intelligibility of poems is dependent both upon the structure of our world of things (never wholly clear to us) and upon the darkness within the poet (never wholly clear to himself). That is why poets speak of the necessity which drives them, and which is perhaps no more than the passive aspect of the struggle to understand and utter themselves and their world, while respecting what is mystery and darkness. The practice of their craft carries poets over waters ruled by the whirlwind: practice, deliberate composing of metaphor and image and figure, removal of the obstacles presented by language only half-mastered, in the expectation of the moment, years in the future, when the poetic impulse released by some unforeseen accident will fuse the right words together in the figures of a poem.

38. Niall Sheridan, in his discerning introduction to the collection *The Heavenly Foreigner* remarks that Denis 'shows a rare power of stating abstract ideas and philosophical concepts in terms of poetry.' This cannot mean, of course, that Denis had the abstract ideas first, expressing them 'poetically' later. Even Valery, for all his intellectuality, does not perform that undesirable feat.

39. In my experience of Denis, I never found him either a philosopher or a theologian. He never accepted, could he avoid it, the form of argument: "I like a discourse from which the middle terms have been dropped," he would say.

He was, I feel sure, intelligent rather than intellectual in type. During his student days he appeared to live as if he were drowning in an intense and varied sensuous flow, neither purely introverted nor purely extroverted. Outside, he could barely see the wood for the trees;

within, all, all was important. Soon enough, as the poem 'Victory of Samothrace' reveals, the flux clarifies sufficiently to allow for glimpses of warring tendencies and loves. The different simultaneous levels of poetry present in Denis's poetry reflect the permanent situation of conflicting loves, in which he discovered the problem of his own life, in solving which poetically he vindicated (his own word) his career as a poet. Let us follow the vein:

> ...timid traveller trailing slow steps about and about
> considering which route he shall take at the crossing of ways.
> — 'O Paltry Melancholy', p. 111

> The wind pads almost noiseless like a cat
> Do not reject its suave caresses, Heart.
> — 'The Alembic', p. 93

> Trifler of grace, from surrender shrinking,
>   And frenzy of streets.
> — 'Gradual', p. 97

> For compromise with love defiles youth ever
> Content is hollow and vile it will remain
> — 'Communication From The Eiffel Tower', p. 105

> In gentleness who not answer
> The shy friendly nudging
> Of that insistent stallion?
> — 'Est Prodest', p. 46

> Night O clearer than the day
> Because the objects of love are visible.
> — 'Communication From The Eiffel Tower', p. 105

> Something there was other
> Always at my elbow,
> I sang, hunted and hated one;
> He sings, hunts and hates me...
> — 'The Heavenly Foreigner', p. 30

Young men will not name the beloved object for fear of
        degrading it.
Mental prayer is the highest . . . And just that point
Which is only and nothing else yourself
Is that point, is that which I love
With no words for it.
                        – 'The Heavenly Foreigner', p. 29

Out of the struggle between possible selves of desire and the discover
able self-destined to its best love, slowly (*Experience teaches, you know.*'
– 'Adam's House', p. 115), slowly Denis disposed all his loves in order,
nothing abstract in the process, all worked out in the man himself:

Praise and recrimination sit well on us
Whose quality's defined by life and death;
But nothing, neither life or death adorns us
Like adoration of our Lord, the Christ,
No buildings, no culture of roses, no bridges
        Like the majesty of Christ.
                        – 'The Passion of Christ', p. 14

Denis had been a lover from the beginning, a lover torn between love
and love who told his loves no lies. His palm is to have uttered his love
of Christ – the substance ultimately of his poetry – in English, thus
now freeing that language from the obstacles which it opposed, when
Denis began writing, to the expression of such a love. Thus he
occupies, in the universe of poetry, the pole opposed to that occupied
by another Irishman of genius, one formidable among the formidable,
whose Malone, whose heartbreaking Malone on his death-bed gives a
transitory abode to the hatred and the vengeance opposed to love:

Laissez-moi dire tout d'abord que je ne pardonne à personne. Je souhaite à
tous une vie atroce et ensuite les flammes et la glace des enfers et dans les
exécrables générations à venir une mémoire honorée.
                        – Samuel Beckett, *Malone Meurt*

40. In conclusion, let the Montaigne whom Denis so often spoke of
approvingly speak for me a final word about my friend:

Il avait son esprit moulé au paron d'autres siècles que ceux-ci.
                        – Montaigne, 'De L'Amitié'

Pickings & Choosings

– Dennis O'Driscoll selects recent pronouncements on poets and poetry

"Being everywhere at once while going nowhere in particular is what poets do."
– Adam Gopnik, *The New Yorker*, 23 September 2002

"Poetry is weirdly utilitarian, because it's so distilled – in less than five minutes, you can read a poem and have an *experience*."
– Deborah Garrison, *Kansas City Star*, 19 January 2003

"The poem is an escalator. The novel is a racing car. It has to go quicker and it eats up the road."
– Craig Raine, *Thumbscrew*, Nos. 20 - 21, 2002

"Prose is like TV and poetry is like radio."
– Simon Armitage, *Times Educational Supplement*, 2002

"In prose, the connective tissue is allowed to show; in poetry it is subverted, subtracted, made invisible, suggested."
– Stanley Plumly, *Atlantic Unbound*, 8 January 2003

"The novel's timespan is different to that of the poem: a poem may infold or implode, a novel stretches out."
– Vona Groarke, *The Irish Times*, 21 September 2002

"Poetry's advantage over prose is its ability to interest us all over again at each re-reading. Its memorability never precludes surprise."
– Peter Porter, *The Age*, 26 August 2002

"Poetry rises out of prose and longs to return to it. It is in the tension of the longing and return that poetry, a language that sounds better and means more, exists."
– Charles Wright, *Orlando Sentinel*, 10 October 2002

"I think a lot of poets can feel like they're writing into a vacuum. Maybe there's an urge to write prose because at least you know it will reach a wider audience."
– Paul Farley, *The Observer*, 26 January 2003

"As long as a poet sticks to the writing of poems, he is socially harmless. But the volatility of the poetic mind expressing itself in prose, with its dangerous social dimension, threatens everyone."
– Harry Clifton, *The Irish Times*, 11 January 2003

"A piece of writing (has) to use sound, resonance, syntax. Imagination has to hover over it. It has to be decorated, but not over-decorated. It has to seek memory, but it has to also prod memory. It has to create the actuality, and also create the utopia that one must try to find through the actuality."
– James Liddy, *The Burning Bush*, Autumn 2002

"Poetry is more than the shape of its verse, it's more than its line-turnings, and its pirouettings. It's a combination of some form of truth, wisdom, and a new way of seeing it, of saying it – as a refreshment of what you know."
– Seamus Heaney, *The Independent*, 31 October 2002

"Poems show us that we are both more and less than human, that we're part of the cosmos and part of the chaos, and that everything is a part of everything else."
– Julia Casterton, Poetry*news*, Winter 2002 / 3

"Poetry speaks to something in us that so wants to be filled. It speaks to the great hunger of the soul."
– Lucille Clifton, *Baltimore Sun*, 29 September 2002

"Poems can be remarkable, virtuoso performances, but if the author hasn't trembled before writing itself, hasn't been inspired by more than the desire to write something, the reader too will not tremble, will not be inspired, will not be tempted to place the book under her pillow."
– Tatyana Voltskaya, *Modern Poetry in Translation* No. 20, 2002

"Don't poetry readers expect to be challenged by the complex negotiation in a poem between the drive to self-expression, the revelatory impulses of language, and the impersonal drama of form?...What else is a poem if not an experiment?"
– John Hartley Williams, *Poetry London*, Autumn 2002

"As poets we lag behind the rest of Europe, in terms of innovation, interpretation and imagination, by roughly sixty years."
– Fred Johnston, *Books Ireland*, February 2003

"Each poet who is seriously exploratory keeps rebelling against his or her own framework of ideas. Many such rebellions are necessary to keep one's art alive."
– Mark Halliday, *The Writer's Chronicle*, February 2002

"The translator's knowledge of *language* is more important than their knowledge of *languages*."
– Jamie McKendrick, Poetry*news*, Winter 2002 / 3

"Translation of poetry is, if it is any good, first and foremost poetry."
– Charles Tomlinson, *Poetry Review*, Winter 2002 / 3

"Scotland's national bard, Robert Burns, brings more than £157m a year into the country…Spending in the Burns supper season on haggis, shortbread and other edible delights equals £1.2m. Another £300,000 comes from other spending like paying pipers and kilt hire."
– *BBC News Online*, 24 January 2003

"Poets are infinitely corruptible; but the trouble is there aren't people around to corrupt them – there are plenty of Fausts around but no Mephistopholes to be seen."
– Peter Porter, *The Age*, 3 September 2002

"The rewards of writing poetry are so little in terms of public life and career that it is the poetry, and the act of poetry alone, that sustains a poet through life."
– Thomas McCarthy, *Cork Literary Review*, Volume IX, 2002

"It's a pity to put a poet in a job that somebody else can do."
– Les Murray, *The Irish Times*, 22 June 2002

"There's nothing wrong with romanticizing the working man, except it's usually the work of a deskbound poet whose nearest brush with hard labor comes, these days, from what he sees in the movies."
– William Logan, *The New Criterion*, December 2002

"Poetry is my larder, my safe and secret place in which to store myself…Not that I believe one is a poet from one moment to the next; it's not like being a banker or a fisherman. Perhaps one is a poet with gaps."
– Alice Oswald, *The Daily Telegraph*, 22 January 2003

"The value of a poetic method doesn't lie in its accuracy or plausibility. The test is simple: Does it produce interesting poems?"
– Mark Scroggins, *Parnassus*, Volume 26 No. 1

"In a poem there is no past; at its inception, everything has yet to be done, felt, imagined."
– Calvin Bedient, *Parnassus*, Volume 26 No. 1

"The warning voices of poets must be carefully listened to and taken very seriously, perhaps even more seriously than the voices of bankers or stock brokers. But at the same time, we cannot expect that the world – in the hands of poets – will suddenly be transformed into a poem."
– Vaclav Havel, *New York Review of Books*, 24 October 2002

"The personal lyric is omnipresent in human cultures because it serves an essential function: to assist in the survival of individuals as they undergo existential crises."
– Gregory Orr, *American Poetry Review*, May / June 2002

"In times of crisis people gravitate to the high rhetoric of poetry because it seems to ennoble us."
– Lucia Perillo, *American Poetry Review*, September / October 2002

"The ceremonial poem requires more of a public voice…The subject matter controls the poem. When I write for myself, I'm trying to escape the subject matter."
– Billy Collins, *The Indianapolis Star*, 18 September 2002

"I asked John Ashbery once in a mutual interview, 'Is there a hidden meaning in any of your poems?' and he said, 'No, I wouldn't put one out there because the reader might find it.'"
– Kenneth Koch, quoted in *Poets & Writers*, September / October 2002

"People find poetry difficult because they're looking for hidden ideas in it but the real purpose of a poem is emotional resonance. If poetry wasn't fundamentally emotion then it wouldn't need to be written in rhythm and with imagery. It's in the wrong form if you're writing basically about ideas."
– Robert Gray, *The Age*, 25 August 2002

"We see things as images and metaphors. In that sense poetry seems to be a very natural form of communication."
– Simon Armitage, *The Daily Telegraph*, 27 July 2002

"Poetry comes at things through particulars, by means of images, and it doesn't deal so easily with generalities. Its mode is to cherish without limit. You could say it is an idolatrous art."
– Galway Kinnell, *The New Yorker On-Line*, 9 September 2002

"I want every poem to be clear, sonically charged, immediate, possessed of an interesting story, and resonant with some meaning available to the interested reader."
– Dave Smith, *Poets & Writers* on-line, 2002

"I've often argued that the only skill any writer needs is the ability to see his or her work from the other side. That is, to put him- or herself in the position of the reader."
– Simon Armitage, *The Independent*, 8 November 2002

"Language that excites the reader's interest is accessible, however much resistance it may offer to understanding; dull poetry is inaccessible poetry."
– Kit Fryatt, *Metre*, Autumn 2002

"Poetry has to be complicated if it's going to reflect the world and what the poet wants to say, and not just reiterate what people already know."
– John Ashbery, *Sarasota Herald-Tribune*, 4 December 2002

"Difficult poetry is the most democratic, because you are doing your audience the honour of supposing that they are intelligent human beings."
– Geoffrey Hill, *The Guardian*, 10 August 2002

"Dr Mahathir Mohamad, the Malaysian Prime Minister...is one of many world leaders to have written poetry, such as Saddam Hussein and Chairman Mao."
– Tim Johnston, *The Times*, 31 August 2002

"Generally I approach love poetry as another way of looking at the wide world. The 'you' and 'I' are like two posts holding up a clothes-line. Any image can be hung out there to dry – everything except your dirty washing."
– Michael Longley, *In the Chair*, Salmon, 2002

"How good is their best? / and how good is their rest? / The first is a question to be asked of an artist. / Both are the questions to be asked of a culture."
– Les Murray, *Harvard Review*, Fall 2002

"Too many contemporary poems start small and end smaller. They don't bite off more than they can chew – they bite off so little they don't need to chew."
– William Logan, *Contemporary Poetry Review*, August 2002

"Too many would-be poets mistake sincerity of utterance for artistic achievement. Too many assume that revelations about an authentic self justify their writing."
– John Lucas, *The Way You Say the World*, Shoestring Press, 2003

"Poetry prizes are now the vehicle of literary reception. Control the prizes, and you control the culture of reception."
– Michael Schmidt, *PN Review*, September / October 2002

"What is it that makes a bad poem? Well, it flinches in the face of crisis. It seeks refuge in platitude or cliché, or even in Beauty with a capital B."
– Alan Shapiro, *Atlantic Unbound*, 30 May 2002

"What the audience wants to hear are not your poems, but what you *think* of your poems."
– Hugo Williams, on poetry readings, *Times Literary Supplement*, 13 December 2002

"Many of those at a reading are poets themselves, so that there is a tremendous ego buzz – sort of a 'Why is he/she up there instead of me?' Then too, some may go just to get drunk or pick up a date."
– Dave Eberhardt, *New York Times*, 22 December 2002

"Poems about sex face the same (if greater) challenge as poems about fine meals or the Grand Canyon: since the experience in question doesn't require special verbal skill to make it pleasurable or interesting, the plain style can seem pointless, while elaborate metaphors risk comic overkill."
– Stephen Burt, *New York Times*, 15 December 2002

"For a late-night show on Five, the follies demanded...are surprisingly innocuous, ranging from wearing a thong to reading poetry."
– TV Listing, *The Sunday Times*, 26 January 2003

"A Selected Poems is like a clock awarded by an affable but faintly impatient employer. It means it's later than you think."
– Sean O'Brien, *PBS Bulletin*, Winter 2002

"Divisions according to gender should apply only to changing-rooms and public toilets – because of natural bashfulness. In poetry, there is nothing to be ashamed of."
– Aleksei Alekhin, *Modern Poetry in Translation* No. 20, 2002

"A bad line-break is a killer, like air in the blood..."
– Glyn Maxwell, *Times Literary Supplement*, 5 July 2002

"Quite apart from measles, mumps, chickenpox and scarlet fever, the family was abnormally prone to fevers, ingrown toenails, sprained or broken bones, sinister rashes, infected jaws, bronchial troubles, septicemia and throat bugs."
– Hilary Spurling, on W.B. Yeats's family, *New York Times*, 20 October 2002

"Poet Laureate Andrew Motion has admitted to using chemical stimulation to help him write poetry – a daily cup of cold remedy Lemsip...A spokesman for Lemsip manufacturer Reckitt Benckiser reassured users: 'It is fair to say that it doesn't cause poetry in most people.'"
– Report, *BBC News Online*, 15 October 2002

Thomas Kinsella in Interview with Michael Smith

MS: Has the poet, as poet, a social function?

TK: Currently, in 'Western' society, I believe not. It would be hard to find anyone whose work is less required. As compared, for example, with the poet in Irish society in earlier times, when the bardic order fulfilled virtually an administrative function for the Irish aristocracy, helping to keep the ruler and the kingdom on a proper path and maintain a stable situation.

Poetry – any art – has a psychic function, fulfilling a need in the individual artist, so that it would be produced even if there was no immediate audience. Pursuing that aspect would be another matter... But the arts also have a function that varies with the society in which they find themselves: playing a major role in religion, with music, poetry, architecture and the graphic arts; entertaining the aristocracy, with baroque music or court poetry; vital public entertainment at certain special times, with ancient Greek, medieval and Elizabethan drama; or psychological discovery, with the Romantics.

We are in a blank time: drained of beliefs and values, stunned by marvellous technology in the service of miscellaneous mass entertainment. The arts are divided, between those that have agreed to serve and those that have moved to the edge. The significant poetry of the time is, I believe, at the edge, fulfilling virtually a biological function. To speak passively: guarding the basics which, for the time being, count for nothing in the outer world. But, to speak dynamically: fulfilling what might be called an evolutionary function, at the global forefront with other creative efforts – in the physical sciences and in metaphysics; in psychology, archaeology and mathematics – which are making the significant human difference.

The difference is understanding. Which (one has to believe) will ease the wearisome, and apparently unending, effort toward the eventual ascendancy of the humane. But pursuing that, too, would be another matter.

MS: What influenced you to move on from your very accessible and traditionally elegant early work to the more tortuous and troubled later poetry?

TK: This is a fixed idea that I have come across in a few places. It is really not borne out by a reading of the poems. My poetry has always proceeded on two fronts. There is a kind of straightforward communication, as in those 'elegant early' poems, and in poems like 'Nightwalker', in 1967; 'The Messenger' in 1978; 'Poems from Centre City', in 1990; or 'The Pen Shop', in 1997. And there is an inward impulse, more exploration than communication – mining for the material: material that gives itself up with difficulty. My first books included poems of this kind, concerned with the psyche, preceding the accessible poems. The first poem in the *Collected Poems*, 'Echoes' from *Poems* (1956), could be called 'tortuous and troubled'.

Some of the early poems like 'Midsummer', 'Soft, to your Places', 'A Lady of Quality' or 'In the Ringwood' were really exercises; the emotion and the sensual content profound and real, but the forms and modes, diction and tone, borrowed from admired models: Yeats or Auden (in some cases particular poems of his) or folk ballads. These were followed not by the 'tortuous and troubled later poetry' but by a long phase of development, with the borrowed modes needed less and less and the poems going about their business in their own way – and I think perfectly clearly. Poems like 'Chrysalides' or 'Dick King' in *Downstream* in 1962, or 'Westland Row 'or 'Ballydavid Pier' in *Nightwalker and Other Poems*, in 1968. And tortuous when required – as in 'Wormwood'. There is nothing inaccessible about this poetry.

The 'troubled' later poetry that is part of the received idea really begins with *Notes from the Land of the Dead* in 1972. This is a special book, dealing in origins, ritual and sacrifice. *Songs of the Psyche*, published in 1985, is another special book, dealing in intimate psychic things. These books are in addition to the accessible work. They don't replace it. And special as they are, they contain much accessible poetry. In *Notes from the Land of the Dead*, 'Hen Woman', 'The High Road', 'Ancestor' and 'Tear', among others. In *Songs of the Psyche*, the three 'Settings'; also 'The Little Children', 'Brotherhood' and 'Talent and Friendship'; and numbers 5, 7 and 8 (at least) of the 'Songs' themselves – taking it that dream and myth are valid matter. In *Personal Places* or *Poem from Centre City*, published in 1990, poems like 'Brothers in the Craft', 'In Memory', 'Administrator', 'Social Work' or 'The Stranger' seem perfectly clear – if troubled by experience.

As to accessibility, the source of the current use of the word is the received idea that Seamus Heaney's poetry is totally accessible. This is equally unreliable, and not borne out by a reading of the poems, especially in the later books, where entire poems are inaccessible: 'Wolfe Tone' or 'A Shooting Script' in *The Haw Lantern*; 'The Journey Back' or 'A Royal Prospect in *Seeing Things*; and frequent images and stanzas, in themselves and in their relation to their context.

What is needed is that scarcest of things in dealing with poetry, especially contemporary poetry: precise reading, with no fixed ideas.

MS: You have translated extensively from Irish. Did you ever consider writing poetry in Irish? An Irish writer has a relationship with Irish, whether it is one of ignorance or engagement: could you comment on the relevance of this to the present Irish literary scene? For example, one distinguished writer in Irish, who shall be nameless, in correspondence with me has been scathing in his analysis of what he perceives as the exploitation of Gaelic material by poets with little or no Irish to give an exotic cachet to their writing. I know that for you it is a completely different matter, but do you think there is any justification for this view?

TK: My first writings, of any kind, were in Irish. With other enthusiasts, straight from school, I established an Irish-speaking society with its own journal, and provided much of the contents myself in a fluent Christian Brothers' Irish, polished by visits to the Gaeltacht. This phase continued for some years, during which I retained my simple enthusiasm, with the Irish version of my name, and with no particular interest in literature – in any language – and no idea of becoming a writer.

A number of accidents came together: meetings with students of literature in UCD, where my own studies in science had aborted; coming upon the poems of WH Auden, and being struck by their relevance to real life, after the false world of our poetry studies in school. Above all, finding Joyce's *Dubliners* – the opening paragraph of 'Araby', electrifying in its accuracy and immediacy. I *had been there*, every day... Out of the depths, a first response. Sitting with pencil and paper in a yard in Basin Lane. And when it came, the first expression of real feeling was in English.

Nationalist enthusiasm (to call it that) gave way to real need. But it did not disappear. Linguistically and in substance, mine is a dual heritage: a life lived in English in childhood; in English and Irish in my early school years; wholly in Irish in secondary school, studying other subjects 'through the medium of Irish'; and working for a whole career in English in poetry, and with the literature in Irish from its beginnings.

Your 'distinguished writer in Irish, who shall be nameless'. (Why nameless, I wonder, unless the comments have to do with me?) I have seen the sort of thing in question: one of the Northern poets stirring-in a poem in Irish among his versions from the French; an 'eminent critic' flourishing a detail of Irish grammar in a review in an English paper. But it is a different matter, and a questionable one, accusing poets, or anyone else, 'with little or no Irish' of 'exploiting' Gaelic material. As though a knowledge and use of Irish were a licence for dealing with Irish material. The only licence needed is a knowledge of the material – in translation, if it has to be – and the integrity of the work. That this is so is a result of Irish history, of the country's dual tradition. My book *The Dual Tradition*, published in 1995 by Carcanet Press, deals with this matter – and with most of the other things we are discussing.

MS: Would you agree that your strong nationalist values put you out of favour with the Establishment here at a time when the political situation in the North seemed to demand accommodation by the South. In other words, do you think you ran foul of the revisionists? It is generally accepted here in the South, if not in the North by Unionists, that you are not and have never been an IRA sympathiser; and yet it seems that your strong sense of being rooted in Irish, indeed Gaelic culture, has contributed to your comparative neglect in Ireland because of the perceived political 'necessity' or 'expediency' of 'ungreening' Irish nationalism. Have you any views on this?

TK: These are large questions, requiring an amount of historical background in the answer. I would point again to *The Dual Tradition*.

The Northern question, while it is a large question, is a simple one, having to do with justice. I am not, and have never been, a Unionist sympathiser. I reject prejudice, brutality and injustice. It is clear that I have to accept them as part of the human character – 'the malice and greed of the species'. But I don't understand them.

And I reject violence as a means towards anything. In most of its aspects – the masked expression of provincial bigotry and religious prejudice, for example – it passes my understanding. But I would understand it as a defensive last resort in certain circumstances; and if I were a brutal bigot pushing hard 1 would always be mindful of that aspect. I wrote the following in 1979, in a commentary on *Butcher's Dozen*, and I believe it still:

> Northern Ireland is a state founded in injustice. It was established during a suspension of democratic process in Ireland – a suspension forced on the British Government by the Unionist minority. Its borders were fixed so as to contain the maximum area and resources over which that minority, on a return to democratic process, would remain a controlling majority.
>
> It is a state maintained in injustice, the artificially created minority North of the border being repressed and discriminated against for more than fifty years, while successive British Governments have ignored their responsibility in the matter.
>
> *
>
> Violence is terrible, but it is not inhuman. In political terms it is the final response to unredressed injustice. And no amount of opposing violence will make it go away – only the removal of its causes. The British authorities have chosen, for passing expediencies in their own 'larger' politics, to evade the treatment of awkward, deep-seated causes in Ireland. This is nothing new on their part. But it was cause for great discouragement that politics in the Republic should have returned, under the Coalition Government of the middle 1970s, to a Redmondite posture, accommodating the British authorities in their evasion. Real issues during this crucial period were narrowed or abandoned in an atmosphere of stylish debate and selective formulations uncaring of (it seemed, finally, unaware of) the realities of human behaviour. Politicians in responsible positions urged what amounted to a Violence Eradication Scheme, as though Violence were a contagious disease curable by the elimination of infected bodies. Such politicians refused to consider the eradication of the causes of violence, and attempted to prevent discussion of such causes as 'unhelpful' and 'untimely'. It is probable that some of these considerations inspired the Irish electorate in 1977 to reject emphatically a Government grown so unrepresentative.

That reference to the Coalition Government of the time, and to its blurring of the issues, would cover for me the current revisionist point of view. I would not see myself as having fallen foul of the revisionists, but the revisionists as having fallen foul of the facts. The basics were put succinctly, in current terms, in a letter to *The Irish Times* on July 10, 1999:

Sir,

David Trimble has rejected the Blair/Ahern formula for setting up the new devolved government of Northern Ireland because he was being asked to "sacrifice democratic rights for expediency".

Surely he can live with such a request. The statelet of Northern Ireland was set up undemocratically as an expedient to avert violence by unionists; it has been run ever since by the expedient of gerrymandered constituencies. The democratic rights of Catholics have been ignored and their protests countered by the expedient of Orange pogroms promoted by the rantings of religious fundamentalists.

As a unionist politician and an Orangemen Mr. Trimble is well-used to sacrificing democratic rights for expediency – other people's democratic rights.

Trimble and unionists in general have every right to fear and mistrust the IRA but the Provos were a product of Catholic fear and mistrust generated by loyalist violence and the failure of the RUC to provide protection when they needed it. – Yours, etc.

Douglas Bain,
Newcastle, Co. Wicklow.

Nothing of the revisionist or of the Southern Establishment attitude – and certainly nothing of the uncaring English – is going to help toward an easement of the situation in the North. In the 1920s the causes were historical and political; they are now totally historical and, I believe, incurable. It is interesting, but not politically useful, to debate events and analyse responsibilities: to blame De Valera, for example – when Collins had fought the English to the table – for not going to the Treaty negotiations instead of Collins; to blame the South for fighting the wrong civil war – among themselves – and not continuing the war with England and the North for a United Ireland, as Lincoln fought the South for a United States. The Irish mistakes are permanent, and we are living with their effects. It is a matter of ameliorating those effects. It would be up solely to the Unionist North to take down the mental spikes around their falsified Ulster – shrunken into a corner of a falsified Ireland, where the northernmost county is still in the 'South', so that they can do things by force while still calling themselves Democrats.

There is nothing to lose. The privileged extra that was once at stake has vanished. Understanding would be the first step, as it is in anything. In this case, the understanding that the Northern problem is the leavings of colonialism and of a dead Empire. Understanding is not approval. Approval of the breakdown of the Empire is not required. Acceptance, however, is another matter. This is necessary and could be more difficult, with obsolete loyalties and emotions interfering. But not impossible, once the downright Northern generations have passed – and the revisionists, with their blurring of the facts.

The Northern poet John Hewitt presented the subject completely in his poem 'The Colony': the colonist stranded in Ireland; scorning the barbarian natives; aware of the injustice of dispossession, but justifying this by the colonist's superior use of the land; disposing of the feeling of guilt, and any impulse toward reparation with a condescending righteousness; but worried – knowing the day is coming when the dispossessed will return to claim their rights; settling finally for a common predicament with the colonised:

> this is our country also, no-where else...

Hewitt himself found the next step impossible – the step of acceptance. But Terence Brown, one of a younger generation in the North, introducing the poetry of Hewitt's generation in *The Field Day anthology*, and describing the society they lived in, has managed to look straight at the Northern realities: a 'Northern Ireland of unionist misrule, British misgovernment and sectarian division'. And Brown has allied himself in print with the hope that the Unionists might discover generosity and liberate themselves from the prison of sectarianism.

MS: There is a common impression of you here as a 'loner'. How would you respond to that impression? Did you ever have a sense of belonging to a group of poets? I have heard the view expressed that your isolation in later years was the result of your lack of concern with the work of younger Irish poets. I know that you showed interest in the work of the late Michael Hartnett from the start; but apart from Michael, it would appear that no other Irish poet of Michael's generation seems to have interested you. Could this be construed as a lack of interest in these poets or an implicit judgement on their work? The reason I raise this question is that some of these poets, such as myself, who admired your work and looked to you for example, felt that you had no interest in them. Though allowing you your right to mind

your own business, I am probably trying to suggest that your withdrawal, or rather your apparent lack of engagement with younger Irish poets in the South, contributed to the dominance of the Northern school. Is this a fair way of seeing things?

TK: On the matter of privacy, there was always an amount of sickness involved – family sickness and sickness of my own.

But I have never belonged to a group of poets. Poetry was always a solitary matter; having nothing to do, for example, with a time in a University. My beginnings there were in science, changing to public administration, with a career afterwards in the Irish Land Commission and the Department of Finance. I made one or two valuable friend-ships with people studying in UCD and running the student magazine, but the important connection was with Liam Miller, starting The Dolmen Press in the early 1950s.

With the Civil Service as background, and my own early efforts at writing, the real reading and experience continued: Joyce and great music; Thomas Mann; early history; the literature in Old Irish. Then America and the twentieth century American poets: Eliot, Pound and others. After our own move to the United States in the mid-1960s I had full time for writing and translating, and for the reading and teaching of the great poetry in English; the subjects always my own choice, the poetry itself and the themes insisting. This is how it continued during my time in the two American universities, and how it has remained.

You mention my lack of concern with the work of younger Irish poets. There is no question of this. There is always, of course, the matter of other things pressing for attention: currently, the reading of certain books on medieval Europe, and the rereading of Milton – understand-ing some of his prose tracts a little better, with sharper mixed feelings, and some further findings on the subject of greatness and the managed self. These are active concerns. And I am busy finishing two books, one of poems and one of readings.

But the primary reason for my not dealing with the younger poets as I have dealt – or tried to deal – with the previous generations is my not feeling wholly at home with the basis on which their work communi-cates. The basic data, processed through my own experience and my understanding of the past, would have a later starting-point, a point after which my judgment grows uncertain and I am glad to hand over to those who have lived through, and processed, the basic matter. In *The New Oxford Book of Irish Verse*, it was with the poets born in the early 1940s – the poetic generation after my own – that was as late as I felt able and willing to deal with.

This has nothing to do with the assessment of individual poems and careers. I am talking about the larger generalities – not about the identification of good and bad art. And, on a matter of detail, Michael Hartnett is not the only poet of his generation included in the anthology. The book ends with the three exact contemporaries: Mahon, Seamus Deane and Hartnett, and I believe I dealt with them fairly in the massive context, together with their near-contemporary Heaney.

I could not agree either, that any neglect or 'lack of engagement' on my part has contributed to the apparent 'dominance of the Northern school'. I can only point to *The New Oxford Book of Irish Verse*, and its equal lack of representation of the younger Northern poets. And to *The Dual Tradition*, where the final chapter deals with the Northern poets magnifying themselves, and each other, in their post-colonial ghetto. And to my own 'comparative neglect', as you call it.

MS: My own impression, especially in my work of editing *Poetry Ireland Review*, is that worthwhile poetry is being suffocated by an unstoppable flow of mediocre verse, the kind of stuff that Geoffrey Hill has described as 'home-video poetry'. Do you think that this is a fair impression?

TK: I think the impression is a fair one, and not only as to the verse, but the quality of critical and general awareness. I have a poem called 'Complaint' on this subject, published in 2000 in *Citizen of the World*:

> The times were bad
>   and we were in bad hands.
> There was nothing to be done,
>   only record.

The poem 'Echo', published along with this, and prescribing standards for the making of the record, is assessing as well the causes of the narrowness and suggesting a corrective response:

> Thou shalt not entertain,
>   charm or impress;
> consider the response
>   or the work of others;

confirm viewpoints,
    satisfy expectations,
leave crucial issues confused,
    or impose order.

These poems to me have a forlorn ring.

We are in a very peculiar phase, totally unlike the time in the late forties and early fifties when I was growing up in a country empty of poetry. There were Austin Clarke and Patrick Kavanagh, and a few fading figures. Now the country is teeming with poetry, and it is hard to know what to make of it. But at any given time, anywhere, most poets are no good, and in Ireland most of the poets are no good... Short term, immediate response doesn't mean anything with poetry. And I would not see any groups or 'movements' as significant. The only encounter that matters is between the individual and the significant ordeal, and I don't find much of that in contemporary Irish poetry. It is possible to write without feeling the need, and I have a feeling of people writing *at* each other at the present time. It is a significant period in Irish poetry, but I think it will find its place in social rather than literary history, with – as always – one or two real poets.

The powerful inventions, and borrowings, of the early twentieth century in literature in English will not go away: the immediacies and the great open forms. Ezra Pound making the pace virtually single-handed; getting rid of the dead shapes – except for special effects, as with all antiques. Even Yeats understood, although it took ten years more in his case, and the horrors of the Civil War. But at the end of the century it seems the slack rhetoric is preferred, as you say. And the careful forms. Michael Longley presenting himself as master of the short lyric. The recent Longley anthology restricting itself to poems in the lyric mode. These things are tiring, through lack of substance. Reality isn't shaped like that. And the reviewers of Heaney's *Beowulf* – annoyed at the overlay of rhetoric, and careful with a different kind of care – are tired.

The current authoritative figures lack scale. There is a confessional piece by Helen Vendler in the *Princeton Library Chronicle* in Spring, 1994, documenting 'A Reviewer's Beginnings': over-excited at her first employment as a reviewer; startled, finding herself accepted on a professional level; taking to her role finally as judge, without really understanding. And recording her limitations, things she is not prepared to review. Pound: 'I don't like Pound', and that is an end of the subject. Which might be understood and accepted as professional bias. But – the entire genre of the novel: 'those peculiar works so furnished with salaries and elections, chairs and tables, diseases and engagements, moors and factories, Wills and indentures. As though one had not enough of these things cluttering up one's own life...'

A notable recent Irish document: a collection of statements from fourteen Irish writers in *The Irish Times* on June 16, 1999 – including the literary editor – recording, in varying degrees of evasion, their total helplessness in the face of *Ulysses*.

In England: Oxford University Press abandoning the publication of poetry, except for profitable special items and anthologies, leaving it to Carcanet Press, an independent press in Manchester, to assume the responsibility.

A major undertaking of *Proiseact Nan Ealan* (The Gaelic Arts Agency), launched in Glasgow and touring internationally: *An Leabhar Mòr*, containing one hundred poems and translations, accompanied by one hundred artworks. Contributors were assured that the artworks are outstanding. As to the poetry, as much of each poem appeared as would fit on the decorated page; the balance at the back of the book.

It is hard, in such times, not to feel isolated.

MS: If you were to re-edit *The New Oxford Book of Irish Verse*, would you do it differently? For instance, you included few women poets. Have things changed in contemporary Irish poetry that would make you change your mind?

TK: I have seen the anthology criticised for its comparative lack of, especially contemporary, women poets. I don't think this criticism is concerned primarily with the poetry, and if I were doing the work again I would not look for different poets on the basis of gender.

There is in fact a strong presence of woman poets in the anthology. The second poem in the book is a powerful anonymous quatrain, a sensual song of loss, from Old Irish. There are many other great poems by women through the centuries, from Irish and in English, early and late.

But I know what is meant by the criticism: that there is no poetry from the nineteenth or twentieth century by women poets. There are two reasons for this. Firstly, that a limit had to be set to the scope of the book; it was decided to end it with poets born about the time of Yeats's death, stretching this a little so as to include Derek Mahon, Seamus Deane and Michael Hartnett, all born in 1941. The other reason is that this left very few women poets for consideration in the nineteenth and twentieth centuries. Taking the names from a random selection of critical books and anthologies – *Modern Irish Writing*, ed. Grattan Freyer (1978); *Irish Poetry After Yeats*, ed. Maurice Harmon (1979); *Contemporary Irish Literature*, by Christina Hunt Mahony (1998); and *Irish Writing in the Twentieth Century*, ed. David Pierce (2000) – the poets who might have been included in *The New Oxford Book of Irish Verse*, and who were not, are Eva Gore-Booth, Juanita Casey, Máire Mhac an tSaoi, Moira O'Neill, Blanaid Salkeld, and Eithne Strong. I would not feel called upon to make any great change.

MS: Is there any particular reason you would care to disclose for your not being a member of Aosdána?

TK: *The Irish Times* conducted a survey of non-members at the end of 2001, and I wrote that it was 'a matter of standards. When I saw the membership, I thought I would be standing for higher standards out of it'.

There are individual members in the various media whom I greatly respect, but the membership as a whole is indiscriminate and filled out with people of no real talent, so that I see no point in membership as a mark of reputation or quality. And the calibre of those in charge; I would have no wish to be assessed by these.

The atmosphere of its establishment – as a clever but marginal embellishment, at minimal cost, in the years of aggrandisement under Haughey – contributed to the same feeling. The very title, taken from a meaningful social and artistic function in Ireland's integrated past and applied meaninglessly, embodies this emptiness.

The only possible point would be financial. And this, too, is meaningless – a parody of the original: providing a welcome addition to an existing income but not a sufficient income in itself.

Notes on Contributors

Michael S Begnal is a poet, and the editor of The *Burning Bush* literary magazine. His collection *The Lakes of Coma* has just been published by Six Gallery Press.

David Butler was runner-up in last year's Patrick Kavanagh Award. His translations of Fernando Pessoa will be published next year by Dedalus.

Arturo Carrera was born in 1948 in Pringles , a province of Buenos Aires. He has translated texts by Agemben, Passolini, Maurice Roche, Mallarmé, Bonnefoy, Michaux and Penna; and has read his poetry and given lectures in New York, Italy, Canada, Chile, Brasil, Paraquay and Mexico. A winner of numerous literary prizes, his publications include *Escrito con nictógrafa* (1972), *Momento de simetría* (1973), *Oro* (1975), *La partera canta* (1982), *Mi padre* (1983). His latest is *Tratado de las sensaciones* (2001).

Michael Clement began writing after moving to Ireland from South Africa nearly five years ago.

Michael Coady is a previous winner of the Patrick Kavanagh Award; the author of three collections from Gallery; and a member of Aosdána.

Brian Coffey's first book, *Poems,* shared with Denis Devlin, was privately published in Dublin in 1930, and was described by Samuel Beckett as constituting 'the nucleus of a living poetic in Ireland.' His collections include *Dice Thrown Never Will Annul Chance* (The Dolmen Press, 1965); *Selected Poems* (New Writers Press, 1971; and Raven Arts Press, Belacqua Series, 1983); and *Poems and Versions 1929–1990* (Dedalus, 1991). He died in 1993.

Jan Conn's most recent collection of poems, *Beauties on Mad River: Selected and New Poems,* was published by Véhicule Press of Montreal in 2000. Her works has also recently appeared in *The Massachusetts Review, The Antigonish Review* and *Prism International,* among other journals.

Celia de Fréine is a previous winner of the Patrick Kavanagh Award. Her collection *Faoi Chabáistí is Ríonacha* won the Duais Aitheantais Ghradam Litríochta Chló Iar-Chonnachta in 2001. Her poems 'A Strange Kettle of Fish' was a prize-winner in the Bridport Prize 2002.

Maurice Harmon's *The Last Regatta* was published by Salmon in 2000. He is a previous editor of *Poetry Ireland Review.*

Aidan Hayes is widely published in Irish, English and American journals, and is also a translator of Francophone poets and singers. He is a graduate of the MA program at the Poets' House, Falcarragh, Co. Donegal.

Marianne Hennessy, at the time of writing her award-winning poem in the **SeaCat National Poetry Competition**, was a pupil at Our Lady's

Grove Secondary School, Goatstown, Co. Dublin.

Rita Ann Higgins's *Sunnyside Plucked: New & Selected Poems* (Bloodaxe) was a Poetry Book Society recommendation. Her latest collection is *An Awful Racket* (Bloodaxe).

Thomas Kinsella was born in Dublin in 1928. He attended University College,Dublin, and after years working in the Civil Service he devoted himself fulltime to writing, teaching for many years in the United States where he now resides permanently. He was a director of the Dolmen Press and the Cuala Press. His *Collected Poems* came out from Oxford University Press in 1996, and was later re-issued (with revisions) by Carcanet. Apart from his original poetry, he has also translated extensively from Irish.

James J McAuley's poems have appeared recently in the *Out To Lunch* anthology and *Writers Forum* (U.S.A.) He reviews poetry occasionally for *The Irish Times*.

Hugh McElveen (cover photograph) works as an educator and photographer. The cover image, 'Curlew Skull', is taken from a work in progress. The series would not be possible without the support of Finbar McCormack and Catherine Boner of the Queen's University, Belfast.

Manus Joseph McManus won third prize in the Strokestown Poetry Competition, 1999. He has also won awards for his short stories.

PJ McNally has won prizes in the Dun Laoghaire Library Service Poetry Competition and in a short story competition sponsored by Telecom Eireann. He is currently working on a novel.

Paul Muldoon was born in County Armagh, and educated in Armagh and at the Queen's University of Belfast. His most recent collections of poetry are *Poems 1968-1998* (Faber & Faber, 2001) and *Moy Sand and Gravel* (Faber & Faber, 2002). A Fellow of the Royal Society of Literature and the American Academy of Arts and Sciences, Paul Muldoon was given an American Academy of Arts and Letters award in literature for 1996. Other awards include the 1994 T.S. Eliot Prize and the 1997 *Irish Times* Poetry Prize. He has been described by *The Times Literary Supplement* as 'the most significant English-language poet born since the second World War.'

Paul Murray lives in Rome. His fourth collection, *These Black Stars*, will be published later this year by Dedalus.

Anna Ní Dhomhnaill won second prize last year in *THE SHOp*'s competition for the translation of Irish-language poetry into English, with 'Circle of Life', a translation of Cathal Ó Searcaigh's 'Rothaí Móra an tSaoil.' She is a full-time translator in and out of Irish and other European languages, and a tutor on the MA course at the Poets' House, Falcarragh, Co. Donegal.

Hugh O'Donnell won the Crann Poetry Competition / Féile Shamhna na gCrann in 2002. His collection *Roman Pines at Berkeley* was published by Salmon, and a second collection is pending.

John O'Donnell is a previous winner of the Hennessy Literary Award for Poetry, and the Listowel Writers' Week Prizes for Best Poem and Best Collection. His first collection, *Some Other Country*, was published by Bradshaw Books in 2002.

Mary O'Donnell is a poet and novelist. Her publications include *Unlegendary Heroes* (Salmon, 1998) and *The Elysium Testament* (Trident, 1999). She is a member of Aosdána.

Dennis O'Driscoll's recent publications include a selection of reviews and essays, *Troubled Thoughts, Majestic Dreams* (Gallery, 2001) and his sixth collection of poems, *Exemplary Damages* (Anvil, 2002).

Eoghan Ó Tuarisc's *Lux Aeterna agus Dánta Eile* was published posthumously in 2000 by Cois Life. A poet, dramatist and novelist, he died in 1982.

Augustus Young was born in Cork and worked in London as an epidemiologist. He now lives in France. He has published eight books of poetry. *Light Years* (London Magazine Editions, 2002), a chronicle in prose, has been widely and enthusiastically reviewed in Ireland and the UK. He is currently working on material relating to 'storytelling'.

Erratum eile: The title of Paul Grattan's debut collection, incorrectly listed in a biographical note to *PIR* 74, is *The End of Napoleon's Nose* (Edinburgh Review).

Books Received

Mention here does not preclude a review in a future issue.

Sam Burnside, *A Will to Remember*, Linen Hall Library.
Fred Johnston, *Paris without maps*, Northwords *folio*.
Rhoda Michael, *In long connected threads*, Northwords *folio*.
John Miller, *still life*, Northwords *folio*.
John Davies, *North by South: New and Selected Poems*, Seren.
Robert Seatter, *travelling to the fish orchards*, Seren.
Paul Henry, *the slipped leash*, Seren.
Ed. by Sheila O'Hagan, *Cork Literary Review*, Volume Nine, Bradshaw Books.
Ed. by James Doan & Frank Sewell, *On the Side of Light: The Poetry of Cathal Ó Searcaigh*, Arlen House.
Ed. by Slakkie Van Der Schyffe, *Carapace 38*.
John Whitworth, *The Whitworth Gun*, Peterloo Poets.
Valerie Laws, *Moonbathing*, Peterloo Poets.
Allison Eir Jenks, *The Palace of Bones*, Ohio University Press.
Martin Pouliot, *Poemas de familia / Poèmes de famille*, Écrits des Forges.
Martin Pouliot, *Capoune!*, Éditions Trois-Pistoles.
Martin Pouliot, *Commentaires sur le Troupeau par un des Membres*, Éditions Trois-Pistoles.
John Duffy, *The Constancy of Stone*, Nepotism Press.
Gerry Murphy, *Torso of an Ex-Girlfriend*, Dedalus.
Mairéad Manton, *The Mean Eye and the Thinking Heart*.
Ed. by David Pike, *Pulsar: Poems from the Ligden Poetry Society*, Edition 4/(02), December 2002.
Ed. by Christopher Howell, *Willow Springs*, Number 50, June 2002.
Ethna McKiernan, *The One Who Swears You Can't Start Over*, Salmon Poetry.
Patricia Monaghan, *Dancing With Chaos*, Salmon Poetry.
Knute Skinner, Stretches, Salmon Poetry.
Jude Nutter, *Pictures of the Afterlife*, Salmon Poetry.
Ron Houchin, *Moveable Darkness*, Salmon Poetry.
Ed. by Esther Morgan, *Reactions*, Pen&inc.
Cliff Wedgbury, *Eye to Eye* (illustrations by David Wedgbury), Three Spires Press.
Aidan Higgins, *As I was Riding Down Duval Boulevard with Pete La Salle*, Anam Press.
Desmond O'Grady, *The Battle of Kinsale 1601*, Anam Press.
Esta Spalding, *Anchoress: A Poem*, Bloodaxe.
Mary O'Malley, *The Boning Hall: News & Selected Poems*, Carcanet.
Justin Quinn, *Fuselage*, Gallery Books.
Michael Hartnett, *A Book Of Strays*, Gallery Books.

Medbh McGuckian, *The Face Of The Earth*, Gallery Books.

Seán Lysaght, *Erris*, Gallery Books.

Ed. by Todd Swift & Philip Norton, *Short Fuse: The Global Anthology of New Fusion Poetry* (CD incl.), Rattapallax Press.

Eva Salzman, *One Two II: a songbook*, Wrecking Ball Press.

Roy McFadden, *Last Poems*, Abbey Press.

Ed. by Nicholas McLachlan, *80 MPH – A Festschrift For Leland Bardwell*.

Martin S. Dworkin, *Unfinished Ruins* (edited with a Foreword by Bernard J. Looks), YBK Publishers.

Rosemarie Rowley, *Hot Cinquefoil Star*, Rowan Tree Press.

Susan Connolly, *Winterlight*, Flax Mill Publications.

Danni Abse, *Touch Wood*, The Corgi Series / Carreg Gwalch Cyf.

Idris Davies, *A Carol for the Coalfield and other poems*, The Corgi Series / Carreg Gwalch Cyf.

Mike Jenkins, *Laughter Tangled in Thorn and other poems*, The Corgi Series / Carreg Gwalch Cyf.

Ed. by Dewi Roberts, *War: An Anthology*, The Corgi Series / Carreg Gwalch Cyf.

David Oberholzer, *Samsara*, Gwasg Carreg Gwalch.

Michael Senior, *Back from Catraeth*, Gwasg Carreg Gwalch.

Pierre Dubrunquez, *poésie 2002*, No. 95 / Décembre.

Ed. by Asher Weill, *Ariel: The Israeli Review of Arts and Letters*, No. 114, Jerusalem 2002.

Ed. by Robert Minhinnick, *Poetrywales*, Volume 38, No. 3, Winter 2003.

Ed. by David Hamilton, *The Iowa Review*, Volume 32, No. 3, Winter 2002/2003.

Elise Partridge, *Fielder's Choice*, Signal Editions.

Henrik Nordbrandt, *My Life, My Dream* (translated from Danish by Robin Fulton), Dedalus Poetry Europe Series, No. 13.

Eamon Cooke, *Berry Time*, Dedalus.

Jane Kirwan, *The Man Who Sold Mirrors*, Rockingham Press.

Douglas Dunn, *New Selected Poems: 1964–2000*, Faber & Faber.

Ed. by Patrick Galvin, *Southword: Journal of the Munster Literature Centre*, Issue No. 3 (new series).

Cliff Wedgbury, *Beautiful Guitars and Other Poems*.

Seán McFalls, *20 Poems*, Peregrine Press.

Nicholas Allen, *George Russell (Æ) and the New Ireland, 1905–30*, Four Courts Press.

Lachlan Mackinnon, *The Jupiter Collisions*, Faber & Faber.

Ed. by David Herd and Robert Potts, *Poetry Review*, Volume 92, No. 4, Winter 2002/3.

Ed. by David Murphy and Aedin Ní Loinsigh, *Thresholds of Otherness / Autrement Mêmes: Identity and Alterity in French-Language Literatures*, Grant & Cutler.

Michael Farrell, *ode ode*, Salt Publishing.
Andrew Grace, *A Belonging Field*, Salt Publishing.
Geoffrey O'Brien, *A View of Buildings and Water*, Salt Publishing.
Brian Henry, *American Incident*, Salt Publishing.
Ed. by Patricia Oxley, *acumen* 45, January 2003.
Mairéad Byrne, *Nelson & The Huruburu Bird*, Wild Honey Press.

Previous Editors of *Poetry Ireland Review*

John Jordan 1-8   Spring 1981 - Autumn 1983
Thomas McCarthy 9-12   Winter 1983 - Winter 1984
Conleth Ellis & Rita E. Kelly 13   Spring 1985
Terence Brown 14-17   Autumn 1985 - Autumn 1986
Ciaran Cosgrove 18/19   Spring 1987
Dennis O'Driscoll 20-21   Autumn 1987 - Spring 1988
John Ennis & Rory Brennan 22/23   Summer 1988
John Ennis 24-25   Winter 1988 - Spring 1989
Micheal O'Siadhail 26-29   Summer 1989 - Summer 1990
Máire Mhac an tSaoi 30-33   Autumn 1990 - Winter 1991
Peter Denman 34-37   Spring 1992 - Winter 1992
Pat Boran 38   Summer 1993
Seán Ó Cearnaigh 39   Autumn 1993
Pat Boran 40-42   Winter 1993 - Summer 1994
Chris Agee 43/44   Autumn/Winter 1994
Moya Cannon 45-48   Spring 1995 - Winter 1995
Liam Ó Muirthile 49   Spring 1996
Michael Longley 50   Summer 1996
Liam Ó Muirthile 51-52   Autumn 1996 - Spring 1997
Frank Ormsby 53-56   Summer 1997 - Spring 1998
Catherine Phil Mac Carthy 57-60   Summer 1998 - Spring 1999
Mark Roper 61-64   Summer 1999 - Spring 2000
Biddy Jenkinson 65-68   Summer 2000 - Spring 2001
Maurice Harmon 69-72   Summer 2001 - Spring 2002